GW00503748

ISBN: 978-0-9894338-3-9
Cover Design: Jenna Stanbrough

Roho Publishing
4040 Graphic Arts Road
Emporia, KS 66801

www.rohopublishing.com

About Roho Publishing

When Kip Keino defeated Jim Ryun in the 1968 Olympic Games at 1500 meters he credited the win to "Roho." Roho is the Swahili word for spirit demonstrated through extraordinary strength and courage. The type of courage and strength that can be summoned up from deep within that will allow you to meet your goals and overcome the challenges in life. Roho Publishing focuses on the spirit of sport and is designed to inspire, encourage, motivate and teach valuable life lessons.

Dedication

To all the coaches who make running fun. Your positive attitude and passion towards physical activity and running makes a huge difference in creating a lifelong commitment to being physically active. The enjoyment received by your athletes has created lasting positive memories of exercise as well as offered tremendous positive benefits physically, psychologically, and socially. You make a difference in developing not only the physical components, but also the heart and minds of athletes.

Acknowledgements

Thanks to my parents, who were not runners, but the hardest workers I have ever known. The beginning of my running career started as a youth following my dad in walking the pastures looking for cattle. Their support of me through the years has been my greatest inspiration.

My loving wife has supported my running and coaching endeavors ever since we met years ago. Her support of my love of running and coaching has been invaluable.

To my three daughters who are all runners. Watching you run and share my enjoyment of running has been a joy. Being able to coach all three of you will be treasured forever. Thanks for your work on this project. To Jenna for her artistic work in the lay-out, diagrams, covers and reviews. To Bethany and Leslie for their review work

To Bill Stinson, my colleague and friend for many years, for his many ideas games and specifically on how to successfully adapt games.

Thanks to my coaches over the years, John Rees in grades 6-8, Tom Foerschler in high school, and Phil Delavan in college. Your encouragement kindled a lifelong passion for running and physical activity.

Table of Contents

Icebreaker/Team Building

Page	Name	Objective/Description
17	Inner- Outer High Five Team	To learn names of team members and to encourage each other while performing an aerobic warm-up
17	Info Card	To learn information about the team while running aerobically
18	Match Run	To learn more about group members while performing an aerobic warm-up
19	The Run is On	To learn more about group members while performing an aerobic warm-up
19	Jog and Talk	To learn more about group members by discussing a question while doing an aerobic activity
20	Teamwork Lap	To learn team member names by runner placing themselves in alphabetical order as they run
20	Scream team	To see which team can run the farthest while screaming
21	Baby Picture Run	To use a running activity and guess what baby picture belongs to each runner
21	Call of the Wolf	To come together to form a pack during a run by responding to verbal sounds
22	Team Telephone Relay	To focus on teamwork and to demonstrate how communication can break down on a team
23	Giants, Wizards, and Elves Challenge	To run to a challenge spot and gather points based upon the power of the character you choose
23	Rock Paper Scissors Tag	After running to a mid-line, based upon a rock-paper-scissors challenge, one partner chases the other partner back to home base
24	The Story Continues	To be creative and write a fun story with your teammates while running
25	Living History Run	To have fun acting out an historical event with while running
25	Photo Finish	To use a picture to determine which team can have the closest finish
26	Motivational Shape Up	To use and reinforce motivational cue words by running and forming shapes
26	Blow and Go	To take advantage of a windy day and chase paper of different point values that blow away
27	Synchronized Running	To have all runners synchronizing their arms and legs as they run
27	Partner Toss	For two runners to jog a designated course, tossing the ball back and forth
28	Parade Maneuvers	To perform parade maneuvers while running with a group

Warm-up/Cool Down

Tag

Page	Name	Objective/Description
43	Tog-Tag Jog	To start behind runners and tag and/or pass as many as possible
44	Scoring Tag	To run across a field to a goal line and score without being tagged and repeating the procedure for a designated time period
44	Animal Tag	To work with a group in imitating an animal, while another group guesses the animal that is being imitated with the results ending in a chase
45	Rip off Tag	To rip off flags of runners and avoid having your flags ripped off
46	High Five Tag	To tag other runners. If tagged, to perform an exercise
46	Flip Me The Bird	To avoid being tagged by being flipped the bird (ball in sock)
46	Powerball Tag	To see how many runners a tagger (drawn by lottery) can tag in a designated time
47	The Blob	The Blob tags runners and they join the Blob
47	Sharks and Minnows	To run back and forth across a field without getting tagged and becoming a shark
48	Capture the Flag	To find and bring the flag of the opposing team to your territory without being tagged
48	Dragon's Tail	Front person tries to catch tail of opposite team, wearing a dragon's tail
49	Domino Tag	To tag runners and collect dominoes collecting the most points
49	Fox and Geese	For the fox to chase the geese with runners staying on paths created by circles and lines
50	Exercise Tag	To tag runners and the tagged runner does a specific exercise associated with the tagger
50	Cone Chase Catch-up Tag	To run around the cones trying to pass the runner in front of them
51	Circle Tag Slap Back	To run around or through a circle trying to link with a partner
51	Partner Tag/ Couple Tag	Match according to skill, the tagger can tag only their partner
52	Moving Duck Duck Goose	To tag and chase runners around a circle, while the circle is moving
52	Fact or Fiction	Runners run to a mid-line and react to a statement that is fact or fiction by chasing or being chased
53	Pac Man	To stay on the lines while playing tag

Relays

Team Games

Page	Name	Objective/Description
67	Circular Attention	To beat an opponent around a circle and return to the starting position
67	Cyclone	To attempt to get all of one team's runners back to the original starting position around a circle before the other team
68	Card war	To sprint to the middle of the playing field and see who has the highest card
69	Frisbee Softball	To throw the Frisbee into the playing field and see how many team members can score before the defense throws the Frisbee to everyone on their team
69	Aerobic Soccer	To play a continuous game of soccer with two balls and no goalies that promotes continuous running
70	Fitness Kickball	To continuously kick balls and try to run around bases before the fielders can return balls back to a box
71	Luck of the Draw Strides	To perform strides based upon cards drawn
72	Bombs Away	To retrieve a thrown Frisbee and organize a line around the fielding team
72	Ultimate football	To pass a football downfield from teammate to teammate across goal line
73	Soccer Softball	To try to score runners around bases before the other team kicks the ball to everyone on their team
73	Community Kickball	To run as a team after kicking the ball and try to get your entire team around the bases before recording an out
74	Ultimate Frisbee	To throw a Frisbee from teammate to teammate to cross a goal line
74	Speedball	For runners to kick or run the ball down the field for a score
75	Musical Running Hoops	To run until the music ends and find a hoop
75	Fear Factor	To do fun, challenging activities based upon television show
76	Amazing Race	To receive clues and solve tasks based upon the Amazing Race TV show
77	Running Baseball	To play a simulated baseball game based upon the pace that is ran for each interval
78	Running for Par Golf	To run from hole to hole based upon pace
80	Battle of the Orbs	To use a variety of balls and trying to score by running, kicking, and throwing
81	Donnybrook	To hit and avoid being hit by balls with an inner boundary and an outer boundary

Fartlek

Page	Name	Objective/Description
83	Leader of the Pack Fartlek	To have a leader control the pace and distance for each fartlek surge and recovery
84	Blind Fartlek	To surge with the leader of a group that has been determined by a secret draw
84	Timed	To run a fartlek surge for a given time and then run a recovery run for a certain time
85	Indian Style	To run fartlek in single file, with the last runners in the group sprinting to the front
85	Team	To run fartlek in single file, with groups sprinting to the front of the running line
86	Pick off the Back	Fun speed play with a focus on surging away and reacting to a surge
86	Lap Elimination	To stay in the game by avoiding being the last person at the end of each lap
87	Whistle Fartlek	To vary the running speed based upon a whistle blowing
87	Number Fartlek	To have a runner lead when the coach calls their number
88	Catch Fartlek	To simulate a race environment where a runner falls behind and must gradually catch-up
88	Hole to Hole Fartlek	To run hard from the tee to the green on a golf or disc golf course.
89	Scoring Golf	To race from tee to green and score points cross country style
90	Golf Fartlek	To see who can come closest to their running pace running from hole to hole
91	Speedy Disc Golf	To complete running and throwing a disc over a disc golf course in the shortest time
91	Football Lines	To alternate running hard and easy using football field lines
92	Back At Ya	To catch an object and sprint to the front of the fartlek line
92	Destroyer	The group leader tries to surge away from the pack, forcing the other runners to maintain contact
93	Zipper	To simulate a race environment where a runner falls behind and races back to catch-up.
93	Group Up	To keep the team close together during a fartlek workout
94	Russian Tag	To develop both the aerobic and anaerobic systems in a fun tag game

Distance

Page	Name	Objective/Description
95	Formation Run	To form group formations while running
95	Flying Geese	To run together in a V formation like geese flying to achieve a common goal
96	Dog and Cat game	To score points by spotting different animals during a distance run
97	Mark My Way	Allows runners to run on a new course and still find their way back
98	Camera Run	To take pictures and document a distance run
98	License Plate Game	To have fun during a distance run by seeing how many different states are represented by license tag plates
99	Twenty Questions	To have fun while doing a distance run by asking questions to identify a topic
99	Digital Scavenger Hunt	To find items on a scavenger hunt by taking digital pictures
100	Shutter Spot	To run to a location and take a picture with a group and challenge other groups to guess the spot the picture was taken
100	Can I Make A Copy?	To run to a spot, take a picture and challenge other runners to guess where the picture was taken and run to that spot and make a "copy"
101	Run and Pose	To run and pose for a picture and challenge other runners to run to the same spot and pose for a picture
102	Poker Run	To collect cards as a team or individuals during a distance run and see who has the best hand
104	Dice Distance Running	To break up a distance run into different time periods based upon the roll of the dice
104	Distance Bingo	While completing a distance run, fill out a bingo distance running card
108	Explorer Run	To explore the area and find answers about different running locations
108	Stump Jumper Run	To run to locations marked on a map in the most efficient manner
109	Clue Run	To receive clues at different running stations that will lead to the final destination
110	Trivia Run	To solve trivia questions while running from station to station
111	Stagger Run	To challenge faster runners by having them start behind slower runners on a distance run
112	Meet in the Middle	An aerobic activity that uses teamwork and allows better runners to run further

Specific

Page	Name	Objective/Description
113	Predict Run	To see who comes closest to the predicted time
114	Road Rally	For teams to learn how to run at a designated pace
115	Out and Back Pacer	To run the same pace on a course going out and coming back
116	Make it- Take It Intervals	To lead an interval group and achieve the designated pace time to keep on leading the intervals
116	Last Man Counts	For a team to achieve a predicted time by working together to help the last runner run faster
117	Hill Tag	To have fun playing tag and at the same time practice running uphill
117	Gut Buster	To maintain contact while running a fast pace being paced by a bike
118	Pursuit	To catch a runner half a lap ahead
118	Team Pursuit	To work as a team to catch a team half a lap ahead
119	The Breakaway	To work on breaking away and catching up to runners
119	Team Bridge	To work with a group to gradually move up from one group of runners to another group
120	Individual Bridge	To work as an individual to gradually move up from one group of runners to another group
121	Running Tournament	To run an interval workout and work on pace in a fun manner
122	Climb the Pace Challenge Ladder	To challenge a teammate of running pace, with the most accurate runner moving higher on the ladder
123	R-U-N	To challenge teammates in running tasks (similar to a basketball game of HORSE)
123	Check My Speed (with radar gun)	To determine how fast runners can run by measurement on a radar gun. The speed determines the distance run
124	Move Out and Pick Up	To continuously pick up the pace while moving outside one lane after every lap
125	Pacer Lights	To adjust pace based upon feedback given by a teammate
126	Tour De France	Keep track of the time for each interval and keep a running total as the workout goes along, similar to the Tour De France
126	Runner's Pentathlon	To run five events and score points based upon performance

Chapter 1

Introduction

The high school cross country team that I was coaching had been highly successful with several consecutive years of top three finishes at the state cross country meet. It was early in the year, and indications were that it was going be another successful year. The team was working hard, they had put in the off-season preparation and the runners were improving. Therefore, I was surprised when a young lady approached me and said, "I'm going to quit." When I asked her why, she replied, "I like the team members. I like being a part of the team. I like the fun things the team does outside of practice. I like the team dinners. I like everything about cross country, but running!" Unfortunately, the young lady did not continue running with the team, but it got me thinking. I loved to run! Doesn't everyone like the challenge and love the satisfaction of completing a hard workout or run? Why wouldn't running be fun? How could I make running fun? Our team still needed to work hard, get in good shape and be racing sharp to compete on a competitive level. Could "fun" be incorporated into the workouts and at the same time obtain our competitive objectives? What would be fun to the beginning runner as well as the experienced runner? What would it take for runners to say, "Running is fun?" Originally, I focused on making running fun for beginners. If the beginning runner could see how fun running was, and get hooked on running, then harder training could be pursued. Once the beginning runner realized the advantages and satisfaction derived from being a runner, the intrinsic motivation would set in and the fun part would take care of itself. As I incorporated more and more fun running games into workouts, I realized that having fun while running is important at all levels; from the beginner to the experienced runner. I also found out our cross country teams were having fun and were still able to achieve our objectives in the hard workouts, that allowed us to develop peak physical condition and to race at a highly competitive performance level.

Running is a natural activity which can be fun, easy to perform, and can be a lifetime sport. Our human bodies are built to move and specifically built to run. Our legs, lungs, and cardiovascular system effectively work together to enable us to run. If you were to go to any elementary school recess and observe the activity of the children, what would you see? Children playfully running over the playground, keeping active and enjoying the positive feelings associated with movement. Humans were born to run! Running is an innate ability. The numerous positive benefits associated with running have long been documented. It burns calories, builds muscle, and helps create a strong cardiovascular system. With all the positive benefits of running, why is there such an epidemic of obesity and a large percentage of people who do not engage in exercise? To help answer this question, one needs to look at the connection between the mind and the body. The more enjoyable an activity is, the more likely an individual will not only begin a program but adhere to it over a prolonged time period. As a beginning runner adheres to a running program, the body responds, adjusts, and adapts in a positive physiological manner so the running activities become not only easier physically, but our mind is also enhanced in a positive manner. That strong feeling of personal satisfaction and accomplishment that accompanies getting in better physical condition mentally motivates us to continue to adhere to our running program.

The first running boom in the United States began in the mid-1970s, started by Bill Bowerman, the Olympic track and field coach from Oregon. The majority of the runners were middle-aged men who were looking to lose a few pounds and get in shape by running 10-K races. In the late 1990's the second running boom started, fueled by young women with the goals of weight control and good health, with the focus more on finishing races than running fast. The next running boom should feature young people. Teachers, coaches, and parents will need to supply both motivation and opportunities to fuel the new running boom.

The National Association for Sport and Physical Education (NASPE) has designed national physical education standards to develop physically educated individuals who have the knowledge, skills, and confidence to enjoy a lifetime of physical activity.

The running games ideas provided in this book meet the *National Standards for Physical Education* (2004). A student who is motivated to enjoy running meets Standard 3 of participating regularly in physical education and Standard 4 of achieving a health enhancing level of physical fitness. With the satisfaction of personal accomplishment achieved in running, Standard 6 of "values physical activity for health, enjoyment, challenge, self-expression and/or social interaction" is met. The enjoyment of physical development for running accomplishes the objective of those standards in developing physically educated individuals who have the knowledge, skills, and confidence to enjoy a lifetime of healthy physical activity.

In 1995, the National Association for Sport and Physical Education (NASPE) published the original *National Standards for Athletic Coaches*. Those standards were revised and renamed the *National Standards for Sport Coaches* in 2006. Over 100 sport organizations agreed that a core body of knowledge existed from which to develop coaching expertise. There are now forty standards in eight domains that identify the scientific and practical competencies that administrators, athletes, and the public should expect of sport coaches. The *National Standards for Sport* Coaches define: (1) What should coaches know? (2) What should coaches value? and (3) What should coaches be able to do? The standards give direction for coaching educators, sport administrators, coaches, athletes, and their families, as well as the public in regards to the skills and knowledge that coaches should possess. It is imperative that coaches aspire to and achieve high standards. In order to achieve the standards, they must have resources available to assist them in gaining necessary skills and knowledge. The standards encourage individuals to gain the qualifications necessary to coach athletes with diverse skills and potential. Perhaps most importantly these standards maximize the enjoyment, safety, and positive skill development of athletes.

This book addresses numerous domains and standards within the following National Coaching Standards. Specifically, four key domains of these standards were followed in developing the book's activities.

Domain 3, Physical Conditioning: The coach is responsible for implementing developmentally appropriate drills and games and teaching techniques that support athlete development while maintaining safety. The coach should encourage healthful decisions by the athlete to promote a healthy lifestyle. *Running Games for Track & Field and Cross Country* stresses safety and developmentally appropriate games to achieve a healthy lifestyle.

Domain 4, Growth and Development: The coach should be able to recognize the need to modify practice and competitive strategies to accommodate the athlete's age, skill, and fitness levels.

Each of the running games provided in this book has numerous variations that can be applied depending on the runner's age, ability, and fitness level.

Domain 5, Teaching and Communication: The coach must plan and implement organized practices to insure that athletes have positive learning experiences. Using a variety of systematic instructional techniques to provide a positive learning environment, coaches seek to maximize the potential of each athlete. Athletes who are positively motivated through positive learning experiences will also maximize their opportunities for potential development. *Running Games for Track & Field and Cross Country* not only describes each activity, but gives ideas on how to successfully implement that activity in a particular setting.

Adapting Games

A successful coach adapts an activity to both group and individual needs to insure a more positive activity experience. Each sport team has its characteristic needs and skills. Not only must we understand this characteristic concept but adapt appropriately and accordingly to each group's specifics. The following adaptation methods and techniques are outlined as suggestions to ponder when attempting to enhance the learning potential and success of an activity.

Change the space or participation within the playing area.

1. Change the boundaries or the distance.
2. Increase or decrease the number of players.
3. Use equipment that will increase or reduce the range of play.
4. Mini teams and games for more opportunities for position playing.

Change the time or intensity element.

1. Change the walk to a jog or run transition or vice versa.
2. Increase or reduce time periods for a run or rest.
3. Partner sets where one runs, the other rests, stretches, or performs a physical activity.
4. Add additional repetitions for more activity.

Modify the rules.

1. Change the order in relay or team play.
2. Change or add rules in the middle of the activity to "equalize" competition.
3. Add elements of cooperation and problem solving for team bonding.
4. Create exercises for eliminated or waiting players.

As coaches plan running activities for a session, adaptation must be considered a necessary part of the planning process. Appropriate games are a significant vehicle toward enhancing the psychomotor, cognitive, and affective growth of athletes.

Chapter 2

Icebreakers/Team Building
Running Games

Traditionally, icebreakers are activities designed to foster interaction among classmates or team members. They are particularly useful in the initial stages of group development to help promote group interaction. They can also be very effective in providing vital energy to practice. These activities develop strong relationships, helping to bring the team closer together. Running icebreakers can be used very effectively during warm-ups, cool downs, and easy day activities to add to the traditional objective of icebreakers.

Inner-Outer High Five Team

Objective: To learn names of team members and to encourage each other while performing an aerobic warm-up.

Description: Run on the track or develop a loop course. Divide into two groups of equal number. From the starting line, half of the group runs a lap in a counterclockwise direction in the inner lane, lane 1. The other half runs in a clockwise direction in an outer lane, lane 2. Whenever runners meet each other, they must give each other a high five and say their own name while passing each other. At the end of each lap, runners switch lanes and run in the opposite direction. On the second lap as they meet, runners give their teammate a high five and say the teammate's name. On the third lap, as they meet, each runner gives their teammate a high five and says something motivating and encouraging. Runners should run in single file and keep spread out from each other a distance of approximately 25 meters.

Variations: (1) After two laps, the inner lane switches to the outer lane and the outer lane switches to the inner lane.

Equipment: A track is not needed, as cones can be used to mark the lap boundaries.

Info Card

Objective: To learn information about the team while running aerobically.

Description: Each runner writes down a fact about themselves on an index card. The runners form a big circle and on command run to the middle of the circle and show their fact card to another runner. If the fact card is true for both runners, than they trade fact cards and run back to the outside of the circle. For example: If Runner #1 card states, "I like cats" and Runner #2 card states "I like dogs" and they both like cats and dogs, then they exchange cards and run to the outside of the circle. Lap 1= counter clockwise, Lap 2= clockwise

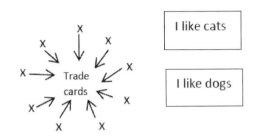

If the fact cards are not true for both runners, they do not exchange cards, but run to the outside of the circle. Runners continue repeating running to the middle of the circle and showing the card to a different person until they have met everyone.

Variations: (1) Runners wait at the outer circle until instructed to start again, instead of continuously repeating. (2) Once runners have met everyone, they should write down a different fact and continue the game. (3) At the end of the activity, all runners come together and each runner shares one fact about themselves to the entire group.

Equipment: Cones to mark circle, 3 x 5 index cards, pencils

Match Run

Objective: To learn more about group members while performing an aerobic warm-up.

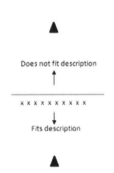

Description: Define a starting line and one turnaround point approximately 30 meters on each side of the starting line. Place the other turnaround point 30 meters on the other side of the starting line. Designate one turnaround point as the matching point and one as the non-matching point. The runners line up side-by-side on a starting line. The first person in line calls out a fact about themselves. Those who match the description will run to the matching turnaround point and back. If the first person calls out, "I have a brother," everyone who has a brother has to run to the matching turnaround point and back. Everyone who does not fit that description will run to the non-matching turnaround point in the opposite direction. After both groups have returned, the next person in line may say something like, "Pizza is my favorite food." Everyone who likes pizza as their favorite food will run to the matching turnaround point and back, while the other group will run to the non-matching designated point and back. Everyone must run one direction or the other.

Variations: (1) The coach picks a runner to call out the statement. (2) The coach calls out the statement. (3) To give runners a rest, the runners who match the statement run, while those who do not meet the fact wait at the starting line and recover.

Equipment: None needed

The Run is On!

Objective: To learn more about group members while performing an activity similar to musical chairs.

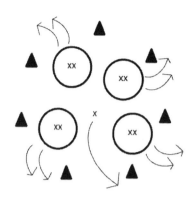

Description: Form a large playing circle marked by cones. Distribute hula hoops randomly within the playing circle. Runners pair up and sit back to back inside a hoop with their partners. One runner does not pair up and is designated to be the standing runner and stand in the middle of the playing circle, but not in a hoop. The standing runner begins the game by saying, "The run is on for…" and finishes this sentence by saying something that is true about them. For example, they can say the "The run is on for anyone who has a pet dog. "If anyone has a pet dog, they must get up and run. Everyone on the team that matches this statement must get up and run (including the runner who called out the statement) one complete revolution around the circle in a clockwise direction and then fill an open position by sitting within a hoop (two people back-to-back in a hoop) that has been vacated by someone for whom the "the run is on. "The last runner standing without a hoop must go to the middle and become the new standing runner.

Variations: (1) Use a different number of runners within the hoop.

Equipment: Hula hoops, cones

Jog and Talk

Objective: To learn more about group members by answering questions while jogging a lap with a partner.

Description: Run on a track or define a running loop. Form two groups of equal numbers in each group. The two groups form two single file lines at the starting line. On an index card, runners write a question for another runner (i.e., "how many brothers, sisters, or animals do you have in your home." or "what is your favorite thing about school?"). Place the cards in a stack near the starting line. The first member of group A draws a card and pairs up with a group B member (who is without a card) and they begin jogging around the track or running loop. For one lap, the partners discuss the question with each other. At the end of the lap, the question card is placed at the bottom of the card pile, and the runner goes to the other group line. Runners will match up with a different runner, draw another card, and run another lap. Continue for a designated number of laps or time.

Variations: (1) The coach writes the questions on the index cards.

Equipment: 3 x 5 index cards, pencils

Teamwork Lap

Objective: To learn team member names with runners placing themselves in alphabetical order as they run.

Description: This works best if the entire team runs together; however, if you have large numbers (over 40), you may want to break down into smaller groups such as boys and girls. The team runs one lap together and runners must place themselves in alphabetical order by last name during the running of the lap. Runners must keep running at all times. At the end of the lap, the runners stop and should be lined up in single file line in alphabetical order. Runners say their last name as a check to see if they were able to place themselves in correct order.

Variations: On subsequent laps, the runners place themselves in alphabetical order by (1) first name, (2) middle name, (3) birthdates, and (4) conclude by placing themselves in some order on a topic (such as favorite movie) without talking.

Equipment: None needed

Scream Team

Objective: To see which team can run the farthest while screaming.

Description: Form groups with three to five runners in each group. Each group should be in a single file line with the first person in each group behind the starting line. On the starting command, the 1st runner in each group starts running and yells as loud as they can on a single breath. Teammates run right behind the yelling first runner maintaining a single file line. When the first runner can no longer yell they move to the back of the group line and continues to run. The second runner on the team takes the lead and starts yelling on a single breath and continues running (the rest of the team continues to run behind the yelling runner). When the second runner can no longer yell, they move to the back of the line and the third runner takes the lead and starts yelling on a single breath. Continue until everyone on the team has yelled. It's fun to see who can go the farthest and scream the loudest! If a group gets to the edge of a boundary, have them turn around and come back.

Variations: (1) Make a continuous relay, when all the runners have had a turn at yelling, the yelling sequence starts over with the first runner. (2) Combine everyone on the team to see how far they can go. Note the distance and go again to see if the team can go further.

Equipment: None needed

Baby Picture Run

Objective: To use a running activity and guess what baby picture belongs to each runner.

Description: Have each runner bring a baby picture. It works best to make a black and white copy of the pictures so the picture doesn't get damaged in the game. Place the pictures on a poster board. Give each picture a number. Place the poster a designated distance away from the starting line, with a number of pencils by the poster. Place papers with the roster of teammates on it by the poster.

On command, all the runners run from the starting line to the poster, pick-up a pencil and roster list and try to match the picture of one runner with their name on the roster. They may only guess one picture at a time. They should write down the picture letter by the roster name.

The runners run back to the start and check in with the coach. If the guess is correct, they run to the poster board and guess another picture. If the guess is not correct, they must run back and guess again and continue until they identify the picture. See who can be the first to match all the pictures with the correct name. When someone has them all right, they have completed the activity and they may be allowed to help other runners. Continue for a designated time period. After the time period is up, gather the runners together and have each runner point out which baby picture is theirs.

Variations: (1) Work in groups. (2) Place the pencils and roster at the starting line and run to the poster board and back to starting line before writing the picture number on the roster name. (3) Use a relay style, with only one runner going at a time.

Equipment: pictures of runners, poster board, pencils

Call of the Wolf

Objective: To come together to form a pack during a run by responding to verbal sounds.

Description: The runners spread out over a designated area. The coach may want to designate where runners start to ensure they are adequately spread out. It works best if the area includes some trees and hills so the runners cannot see each other. Designate a runner to start howling after everyone has had an opportunity to find their starting position. All runners will begin howling like a wolf. Runners will run

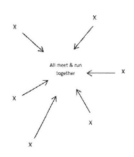

21

toward the howls to all come together as a pack. Once the runners form a pack they should run together for a designated time or distance.

Variations: (1) Divide into groups of smaller numbers with each group having a unique howling call.

Equipment: None needed

Note: The center of a wolf's universe is its pack, and howling is the glue that keeps the pack together. Some have speculated that howling strengthens the social bonds between pack mates. The pack that howls together stays together! Howling also keeps pack mates together, physically. Because wolves range over vast areas to find food, they are often separated from one another. Of all their calls, howling is the only one that works over great distances. Once together the group runs for a designated time together. The strength of the pack is the wolf and the strength of the wolf is the pack!

Team Telephone Relay

Objective: To focus on teamwork and to demonstrate how communication can break down on a team.

Description: Run on a track or develop a loop course. Form groups with four to five runners in a group. The runners for each group should spread out an even distance apart for a relay on a loop course. The coach whispers a phrase into the ear of the first runner of each group at the

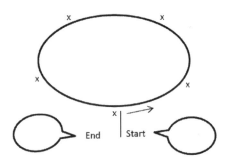

starting line. The first runner then leaves the starting line and runs to the second relay runner on their team and whispers the phrase to that person. The relay continues with the incoming runner whispering the phase to each outgoing runner until the last person finishes. When each runner is done with their individual relay leg they should run back to the finish line and wait for their team to finish. When every team is finished, all the runners gather together and the last person on each relay team repeats out loud to all the groups the phrase that they have heard. Nearly always, the final phrase will be significantly different from what it started!

Variations: (1) Runners do not have to all run the same distance; more talented runners can run further. (2) Run as a shuttle relay. (3) Use motivational sayings.

Equipment: None needed

Giants, Wizards, Elves Challenge

Objective: To run to a challenge spot and gather points based upon the power of the character you choose.

Description: There are three main species of characters, all vying for ultimate power in the forest. The Giants stand tall and stretch their arms high over their heads and growl. The Wizards have magical powers that come out of their pointing fingertips when they say "Abracadabra! "The Elves, have wriggling antennae-like ears (use your fingers wriggling above their heads) and are hypnotizing to any who sees them. Practice with each runner imitating each character.

Form two groups. Define two starting lines approximately 50 to 100 meters apart and a mid-line (challenge spot). Runners line up in two single file lines with one group at each starting line. The lead runner in each line sprints toward the center (the challenge spot). When the two lead runners meet each other at the challenge spot, they give each other a high five, turn around and walk two steps forward, spin back around to face their partner and imitate the character of their choice. Giants beat Wizards (by stomping on them). Wizards beat Elves (by stunning them with their magic). Elves beat Giants (by hypnotizing them with their antennae). The winner of the challenge receives one point. In the case of a tie, each runner receives one-half of a point. Runners are responsible for keeping track of their own points. After the challenge, runners should jog back to the end of their line. Continue for a designated time period. The next runner in line may start running toward the challenge spot when the runner ahead of them is halfway to the challenge spot.

Variations: (1) To break a tie, use rock, scissors, paper. (2) Designate a winner line with the winner of each challenge, jogging back to the designated winner line and the non-winner going to the end of the non-winner line.

Equipment: Cones to mark starting lines and middle

Rock-Paper-Scissors Tag

Objective: After running to a mid-line, based upon a rock-paper-scissors challenge, one partner chases the other partner back to home base.

Description: Form two groups. Define two starting lines approximately 50 to 100 meters apart and a mid-line. On both sides of the midline, mark a run-up line five feet from the midline. Form two groups. Runners line up with one group at each starting line. Each runner should have a partner on the opposing team of similar running ability. Both partners will start at their own starting line at the same time and run towards each other to their run-up line. Once both partners are at the run-up line, facing each other, they count one, two, three. On the count of three, runners show one of the following: rock, paper, or scissors. Paper covers rock, scissors cut paper, and rock beats scissors. The loser turns around and runs back toward their starting line. The winner chases them and attempts to tag them lightly on the shoulder before they reach their starting line. If the runner is successful in reaching their home starting line without being tagged they receive one point. If the chaser tags the runner, the chaser receives one point. Both runners jog back to their original starting line and go again.

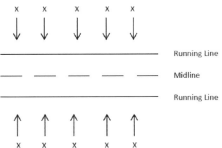

Variations: (1) Both runners sprint to the center line and do rock-paper-scissors. Eliminate the tag portion of the game and score one point to the winner. Both runners jog back and go again. Keep track of the score and play for a number of runs or time.

Equipment: Cones to mark the baseline and run-up lines

The Story Continues

Objective: To be creative and write a fun story with your teammates while running.

Description: Create numbered stations spread throughout a designated playing area. The number of stations created should match the number of runners. At each station in the playing area, leave paper to write on and a pencil. (I recommend leaving the paper on a clipboard, to make it easier to write on). There should be one runner at each station to start the game. Runners will write one line for a story on the piece of paper at each station. The first runner at each station starts the story by writing one line. After writing the line, each runner moves to the next numbered station, reads the previous part of the story and then writes another line of the story. Runners continue going to the numbered stations in chronological order, adding another line to the story at each station. Runners must write their initials after the line they write. Runners are not allowed to write the same thing on every paper. They should write legibly, follow grammar rules and be creative! Continue the game until each runner has been to each station or for a designated time period each. At the end of the activity, all of the stories are read.

Variations: (1) Runners partner up to run and write the story. (2) If you have a large group, you may have multiple people running and writing together. (3) The coach can give ideas for the stories.

Equipment: Cones to mark and number stations, clipboards, paper and pencil for each station

Note: The coach may want to give suggestions on what to write on.

Living History Run

Objective: To have fun acting out an historical event with while running.

Description: Form groups with an equal number of people in each group. Each group will choose a historical event that they will be acting out. (for example: Paul Revere warning that the British are coming). Define the playing boundaries so that the running distances are appropriate to your group. When the group has acted out the historical event for a designated time period, they choose another historical event to act out.

Variations: (1) Give the runners some possible suggestions of historical events to act out. (2) Supply the groups with cards that have information of a summary of an historical event on each one. Have them read the information cards about the historical event within their group and then act out the event.

Examples: Oklahoma Gold Rush, California Gold Rush, Storming of Normandy Beach, A Revolutionary War Battle, Pony Express,

Equipment: List of historical events to act out

Photo Finish

Objective: To use a picture to determine which team can have the closest finish.

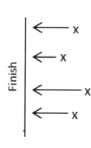

Photographer

Description: Divide into groups with approximately five runners in each group. Each group will need a digital camera. Designate one of the group members to be the photographer for the first round. The other four people in the group will run a designated distance (approximately 100 meters). The objective is to have all of the runners in the group abreast at the finish line, with the photographer taking a picture, a photo finish. After crossing the finish line, the runners jog back to the starting line. In the second round, rotate so another runner in the group is the photographer. Continuing rotating so each person in the group will have a chance to be the photographer. Within each group determine which running round had the closest finish (everybody in the group together leaning across the line). Groups should compare their closest finish picture to the other groups to determine who had the "closest" overall photo finish.

Variations: (1) Runners perform the run all out. (2) The runners or coach can set a goal pace that everyone on the team is capable of running.

Equipment: Digital photo camera or cell phone camera for each team

Motivational Shape-Up

Objective: To use and reinforce motivational cue words by running and forming shapes.

| Word Box | Location Box |

Description: Form groups with five to six people in a group. The coach completes index cards with different motivational words or running words such as "power," "fast", "relaxed", or "strong" on each card. The index cards are placed in a box called the word box. In a separate box called the location box, the coach places index cards that have a location to run to on each card. Each group will run to the location box and one person in the group will take out a location card. The group then runs to the word box and one person pulls out a word card. Everybody in the group should continually repeat the word from the word box as they run to the location. Once the runners reach the location they spell out the words with their bodies. When done spelling out the word, the runners will repeat the cycle by going to the location box, then the word box and drawing more cards. The cards should be placed at the bottom of the pile after they have been drawn.

Variations: (1) Add a third box that indicates exercises to be done at each station after the word is completed.

Equipment: Two boxes, index cards with words and location written on them.

Blow and Go

Objective: To take advantage of a windy day and chase paper of different point values that blow away.

Description: Ever have one of those windy days where you can't keep your hat on or your papers on your clipboard? Take advantage of it by using the wind for an anaerobic workout. On pieces of notebook paper, write down different point values. Form equal size groups and line up on the starting line. The coach holds the flat pieces of paper up and lets the wind catch them. Let the paper get a bit of a head start before you give the command for the runners to chase the papers. The runners work together in groups and sprint to retrieve the papers. After the papers have all been recovered they jog back to the starting line. After each round, record the number of points each team received. Continue for a designated number of times.

Variations: (1) Chase the paper down as individuals. (2) See who can collect the most pieces of paper rather than using point values. (3) Have a different colored paper that is worth more points. Allow the wind to blow the colored paper further than the regular colored paper.

Equipment: Recycled paper—the paper tends to get wrinkled after a time or two so you may need to periodically to replace the paper.

Note: At track practice one day, the wind was really ripping! As I thumbed through the pages on my clipboard, the wind caught them and off they blew. Immediately, the team members started chasing the papers and cheering each other to catch up to the papers. I thought, "what a good workout this could be," thus the blow and go workout!

Synchronized Running

Objective: To have all runners synchronizing their arms and legs as they run.

Description: Divide into groups of four to eight runners per group. The runners in each group line up side by side in a straight line and attempt to synchronize their arms and legs as they run. Start off running a straight line, such as a track straightaway. Runners should run at a slow speed the first few times to practice before they gradually pick up the pace. After a straight line run is mastered, the runners should attempt to run a curve. Place the faster runners on the outside as they will be running farther. It takes a little bit of practice before runners can get the synchronization down.

Variations: Once the straightaway and curves are mastered add some trickier maneuvers such as: (1) a 180 degree clockwise turn, (2) a 360 degree turn, (3) a clockwise 180 degree turn followed by a 180 degree counter clockwise turn, (4) Coaches can judge which group is the most synchronized, giving them 1-10 ratings, similar to Olympic synchronized diving. (5) Emphasize staying close to each other. If each group keeps the line within one-meter distance from each other, they receive a point.

Equipment: None needed

Note: Synchronized diving is in the Olympics, synchronized running may be next! Start practicing it; it could be a ticket to be in the Olympic Games.

Partner Toss

Objective: To have fun doing a team building aerobic activity.

Description: Two runners become partners and will have one tennis ball. From the starting line, runners will jog a designated course, tossing the ball back and forth. If they drop the ball, they must go back to the starting line to start over. The ball cannot be handed off.

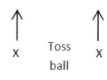

Variations: (1) Pick a topic and each time the ball is passed the passer must say something about the topic. For example, if college names are the topic, every time a ball is passed the passer must say the name of a college. A different college must be used on each pass.

Equipment: One tennis ball for every two people

Parade Maneuvers

Objective: To perform parade maneuvers while running with a group.

Description: Form groups of approximately 10 to 12 runners within a group. While on a run, each group will perform parade maneuvers. Runners should be creative in developing their parade maneuvers. Make sure there is room for the runners to safely perform the maneuvers while running.

Parade Maneuvers suggestions:
- The circle maneuver where everyone runs in a circle that keeps moving forward.
- The figure 8, where runners cut through and cross between each other as the figure eight moves forward.
- The suicide, where three runners run an inner circle surrounded by the other runners running an outer circle in the opposite direction, with both circles gradually running forward.

Variations: (1) After each group has had an opportunity to practice their maneuvers during a designated distance run, hold a culminating parade, where each team can demonstrate the maneuvers that they practiced during the run

Equipment: None needed

Chapter 3

Warm-up and Cool Down

Warm-up refers to the preparation phase at the beginning of an exercise session. Warming up generally involves a period of lower intensity exercise, which prepares the body for more strenuous activity to follow. Running game warm-ups involve performing a running activity at a low intensity before increasing the intensity to the desired level. Adding fun activities to the warm-up and a cool down allows for increased motivation so these important components of the workout can be accomplished effectively.

Mirror Running

Objective: To introduce fartlek running by having one runner mirror the actions of another runner.

Description: Divide the runners into pairs. One partner is designated as the leader. The leader runs back and forth in a designated running area while the partner attempts to stay beside them and mimic as closely as possible the running action of the leader. If the leader stops, starts, and change their pace, the object is for their partner to run along beside the leader as in a mirror and stop, start, and change their pace right along with the leader. Designate a time for the activity (such as 30 seconds) and have the partners switch roles.

Variations: (1) Runners and their partners run to a designated point and return.

Equipment: None needed

Crazy Cups

Objective: To knock down or pick-up cups with your team to see which group can knock down or pick-up the most cups.

Description: Scatter small paper cups around the designated playing area with half of the cups standing up and the other half lying down. Divide the runners into two groups of equal numbers. On the go command, group A tries to knock down all the cups that are standing, while group B tries to stand up all the cones that are lying down. Runners may not knock down or pick-up the same cup two consecutive times. After knocking down or setting up a cup, a runner must go to a different cup. After one minute, stop and count the number of cups knocked down for Group A and all the cups standing up for Group

B. The number counted is the team score. Switch with the roles reversed. Play for a designated number of rounds.

Variations: (1) Form one large group and attempt to knock down or stand-up up all the cups as fast as possible. Keep track and see if the group can improve their time. (2) Spread the cups out over a large area to increase the distance that is run. (3) Use alternative ways to knock down- the cups such as with elbows, feet, etc.

Equipment: Paper cups or cones (you could use two liter plastic bottles)

Cheetahs, Deer, and Elephants

Objective: To simulate running like different animals to acquire what the changing speeds of fartlek feels like.

Description: Runners spread out over the designated playing area. When the coach calls out "cheetah," the runners sprint and imagine they are a cheetah. When "deer" is called out, the runners run at a fast pace (but not all out) concentrating on good form imagining they are a deer running. When "horse" is called out, the runners will run at an easy pace. When "elephant" is called out, the runners race walk imagining they are an elephant, swinging their arms powerfully. When "dog" is called out, the runners will jog. When "turtle" is called out, the runners will walk slowly. The coach/leader should call out fast and slow animals as to allow for both higher intensity running and recovery. This is an excellent activity for introducing fartlek training where runners can feel the difference between changing speeds.

Variations: (1) Incorporate the use of different animals. (2) To progress to harder workouts, increase the length of time for faster animals. (3) To decrease the recovery time, allow less time for slower animals.

Equipment: None needed

Cheetahs, Deer, and Elephants	
Animal	Pace
Cheetah	Sprint
Deer	Fast Pace
Horse	Easy Pace Run
Elephant	Race Walk
Dog	Jog
Turtle	Walk slowly

Whistle Mixer

Objective: While running, gather in groups based upon the number of times the whistle is blown.

Description: Designate a running area. The runners should spread throughout the designated running area and start running at an easy pace. When the coach blows a whistle a certain number of times, the runners get into groups that match the number of times the whistle has blown. The runners must keep running while they form groups. For example, if the coach blows the whistle five times, the runners form a group of five. Anyone not in a group consisting of the correct number within 10 seconds must report to the coach to do an exercise. Continue playing for a designated time period.

Variations: (1) When the whistle is blown, the coach points a direction and all runners run in that direction without getting in groups. (2)When the whistle is blown once, everybody runs north, when the whistle is blown twice everyone runs east, when the whistle is blown three times, everyone runs south, when the whistle is blown four times everybody runs west.

Equipment: Whistle

All Catch

Objective: To communicate and work together while running and tossing balls.

Description: Form groups of 10 or less in a group. Everyone in the group has a tennis ball. Each group should designate the throwing order as to who will be thrower one, two, three, etc. As the group begins to jog in a designated area, thrower one tosses ball one in the air. Someone in the group must catch the ball before it hits the ground. Once ball one is caught, ball one is thrown again and at the same time ball two is tossed simultaneously. Both balls must be caught, but one person cannot catch more than one ball. Next, three balls are tossed simultaneously and caught. Continue tossing, catching and adding balls until all balls are being tossed at the same time. If a ball is dropped, the team must go back to the starting line and begin again. Balls must be thrown simultaneously. It helps if someone in the group gives a command such as "1, 2, 3, toss. "Communication is very important!

Variations: (1) The ball must be thrown to a different person every time.

Equipment: A tennis ball for everyone.

ETA (Estimated Time of Arrival)

Objective: To estimate how long it would take to perform a list of multiple physical activities.

Description: Divide into three to five runners per group. Each group draws an exercise card with a list of five activities and the location where they will perform the activities. Before beginning, the group gets together and estimates how long it will take their group to complete the five exercise stations at the different locations and get back to the start. The group should run together and each person in the group must complete the exercise at each station before the group can move on. Everyone does the same number of repetitions at each station. The team that gets to a station first has the right of way and the other team must wait until the first team gets started. The team that most accurately predicts their finishing time wins. The order of the team activities on each card should be mixed up to avoid all groups going to the same station at the same time. The team closest to their predicted time wins. Runners are not allowed to wear watches.

Examples of Four Groups:

Group 1	
Station 1	30 Sit-ups at the NE corner of the track
Station 2	One lap around the football stadium
Station 3	2 x 100 meter strides on the football field
Station 4	15 Push- ups at the NW corner of the tennis courts
Station 5	Skip 50 yards starting on the SE corner of the football field

Group 2	
Station 1	One lap around the football stadium
Station 2	2 x 100 meter strides on the football field
Station 3	15 Push- ups at the NW corner of the tennis courts
Station 4	Skip 50 yards starting on the SE corner of the football field
Station 5	30 Sit-ups at the NE corner of the track

Group 3	
Station 1	2 x 100 meter strides on the football field
Station 2	15 Push- ups at the NW corner of the tennis courts
Station 3	Skip 50 yards starting on the SE corner of the football field
Station 4	30 Sit-ups at the NE corner of the trail
Station 5	One lap around the football stadium

Group 4	
Station 1	Skip 50 yards starting on the SE corner of the football field
Station 2	30 Sit-ups at the NE corner of the track
Station 3	15 Push- ups at the NW corner of the tennis courts
Station 4	One lap around the football stadium
Station 5	2 x 100 meter strides on the football field

Variations: (2) Run as individuals. (2) Repeat the activities a number of times and determine the cumulative time off the estimated time.

Equipment: Cards with lists of activities and locations.

Dice Running

Objective: To roll dice to see which team performs an activity and which team continues running.

Description: Form four groups with an equal number of runners in each group. Number the groups from one to four. All runners jog on the track or in a large loop. An exercise is called out by the coach (example: 10 push-ups). The dice is rolled by the coach and if the number showing on the dice is one, two, three or four, the group with that number does the activity that was called out. The other three groups continue to jog the circle. When the exercising group is done with the exercise they run after the other runners to catch them. If the number six shows on the dice, all groups do the activity. If the number five shows on the dice, the coach does the activity. Continue for a designated number of loops or time.

Variations: (1) Alternate runners in the group calling out the exercises and the number of repetitions before rolling the dice. (2) Alternate team members rolling the dice.

Equipment: Dice

Visualization Run

Objective: To enjoy visualizing a scenario while running.

Description: The coach designates a running area. Each runner will run for a designated time and act out a dream. The coach may provide a list of possible scenarios. While running, the runners act out what the scenario might look like. For example: winning the Olympic Games, running the Boston marathon, or beating Steve Prefontaine. Encourage athletes to change paces as they run through the visualization. After a designated time period, pick another dream to act out.

Possible visualizations:

- setting a new world record
- anchoring a winning relay
- upsetting an Olympic Champion
- winning the state cross country championship
- outsprinting Usain Bolt

- setting a world record in the 100 meters
- running a sub 4 minute mile
- racing the Kenyans in the steeplechase

Variations: The coach may dictate what visualization to act out with all runners acting out the same visualization.

Equipment: None needed

Number Run

Objective: To find numbered objects in chronological order and to run to the object.

Description: The coach designates a playing area and scatters 20 objects that are numbered 1-20 throughout the playing area. These could be numbered tennis balls, cones, carpet squares, bean bags, etc. Every runner is assigned a number and starts at their assigned number. If you have more than 20 runners, there will be more than one runner starting at a numbered object. On command, the runners start running and search for the next number. They must touch the numbered object and continue to find more numbers in chronological order. Since 20 is the top number, when 20 is reached, the runners will go to number one. Continue the activity until the runners have been to all 20 spots. Repeat the activity if you desire. Runners should be faster the second time since they know where the numbers are. This is a great activity for space awareness and learning how to run in space.

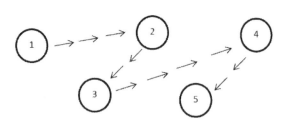

Variations: (1) Time the runners the first time through. The second time through challenge the team to improve the time. (2) Allow runners to move the numbers and place in a different spot, making the numbers more difficult to find. (3) Use the alphabet instead of numbers. (4) Run with a partner.

Equipment: Numbered objects

Warm-up Trail

Objective: To perform different activities as runners run back and forth in serpentine style on the exercise trail.

Description: The coach will make five lines marked by cones and call them warm-up trails. The trails will start at the starting line (trail head) and go to a cone that will be the turn-around point. Trail 1 begins at the far left corner of area. Runners will spread out with an equal number starting at each of the five trailheads. Runners will run down and back on the trail and then

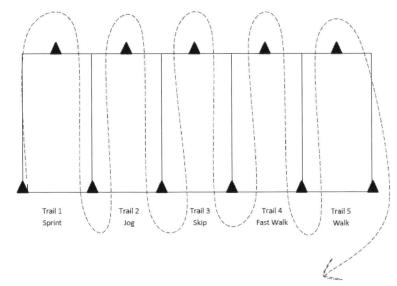

34

move to the next trail. After trail five, runners go to trail one. This is a continuous run, as soon as a runner gets back to the trailhead; they move to the next trail and keep on going. On each trail there will be a specific activity. To help runners remember what activity to do, post that activity on the cone at the beginning of each trail.

Trail 1: sprint down and back
Trail 2: jog
Trail 3: skip
Trail 4: fast walk
Trail 5: walk

Variations: (1) Vary the activities used on each trail. (2) Add an exercise zone at the end of each of the turnaround cones and perform a different exercise on each trail.

Equipment: Cones to mark the exercise stations.

Group Juggling

Objective: To throw balls back and forth within a running group and to see how many balls can be kept going at once.

Description: Designate a running area. Divide into groups of three to six runners in each group. Runners will toss a tennis ball as they run within the designated area. Establish a throwing pattern within the group by starting with one runner holding a ball, and then passing to someone that is not next to them. The group keeps throwing until everyone has received a pass. Add additional balls and try to see how many items the group can keep going as they run. Groups should use the same throwing order.

Variations: (1) Perform the running activity with different objects such as bean bags, rubber chickens, or hula hoops. (2) Make the running course a loop. On the first lap, the group tosses one object back and forth. Each additional lap, add one more object.

Equipment: Tennis balls or other objects, safe to juggle

Exercise Bingo Run

Objective: To complete exercises and fill in an exercise bingo card.

Description: Create a running loop with several stations. At each station, place exercise cards and pencils. Cut up the exercise bingo card to use as the exercise cards. An exercise card will have different exercises listed on them. An exercise bingo card that has exercises instead of numbers will be used. Spread the runners out with an equal number at each station. Each runner will have an exercise bingo card. On command the runners start running clockwise to the next station. As the runners arrive at the station, they will draw a face down exercise card. The runner returns the card to the bottom of the pile and performs the exercise on the card. After performing the exercise, the runner marks with a pencil the exercise they just performed on their running Bingo card. The first runner to get all the areas marked across, down or diagonally wins.

Variations: (1) Fill the bingo card in completely. (2) Runners can pick the exercises they want to do to get a bingo. (3) Perform the activity in groups, with an entire group performing the exercise.

Equipment: Bingo card with exercises shown instead of numbers, exercise cards with different exercises on each, pencils to mark or better yet some small stickers to place on the exercise bingo card.

Exercise Bingo Card

Mountain Climbers 10	Skip for height 2 x 30 meters	Wild Card Your choice of exercise 15 reps	Jumping Jacks 20	Flex and Jump 10
Push-ups 20	Squat Thrusts 15	Arm Circles 10 each arm	Walking Side Lunges 2 x 20 meters	IT Band Stretch 10 seconds
Leg Swings 20	Inchworm 2 x 5 meters	Free	Push-ups 10	Squat Thrust 10
Strides 2 x 100 meters	Lunge Walks 2 x 15 meters	Wild Card Your choice of exercise 20 reps	Heel Walk 2 x 10 meters	High Knee Lift Walk 2 x 15 meters
Wild Card Your choice of exercise 10 reps	Flex and Jump 10	Jumping Jacks 30	Sit-ups 20	Mountain Climbers 15

Popcorn

Objective: To use a fartlek type activity simulating popcorn popping to vary intensity and change of direction during a warm-up run.

Description: This run imitates popcorn popping. Runners should spread out over the designated area. On command, all runners will squat down. The coach waits 10 seconds (the popcorn is warming up) and then blows the whistle several short quick blasts. The first blast signals that the popcorn is ready to pop. Runners will rise to a standing position, extending their arms overhead and shaking them vigorously to indicate the intensifying heat, then start running slowly and as the popcorn warm-ups the runners will increase their speed. Just like popcorn kernels popping in all directions, runners should change directions often. After 10-15 seconds, the coach blows the whistle for stop signal, and the runner's squat down and prepares to repeat the activity.

Variations: (1) Every time the coach blows the whistle, the runners change direction.

Equipment: Whistle

Sport Scenarios

Objective: To visualize and act out a famous sports scenario in a running manner.

Description: Define a running area. The runners will spread out in an area and begin running. When the coach calls out a sports scenario, the runners will individually act out the scenario. After a designated time period, the coach blows the whistle and calls out another sports scenario.

Possible sport scenarios to use:
Winning the Kentucky Derby
Winning the Indy 500
Dunking a basketball
Downhill skiing at the Olympics
Being a golf ball hit towards a hole
Catching a football pass and running towards the end zone for a touchdown
Swimming at the Olympics
Outrunning a throw to first
Riding in a bobsled at the Olympics
Riding in the Tour de France
Outrunning the bulls in the Running of the Bulls

Variations: (1) Each runner gets a turn of calling out a scenario of their choice. (2) Each runner gets a turn of calling out the scenario and acts as the leader that others must imitate.

Equipment: None needed

Hot Potato Run

Objective: To toss a tennis ball back and forth while running and to not get caught holding the ball.

Description: Form groups with three to five runners in each group. Each group will have one tennis ball. On command, the group begins running within a designated area or on a loop course. As they run, they toss a tennis ball (the hot potato) within the group. The goal is to hold the ball (hot potato) as short a time period as possible. After a certain time period, the coach will blow the whistle. The runner holding the ball (hot potato) will do five push-ups. The rest of the group will continue to run and toss the ball in the group. After the runner completes the push-ups, they will catch up to the rest of the group. Repeat the activity for a designated time period.

Variations: (1) Change exercises to do if caught holding the hot potato

Equipment: Ball for each group, whistle

Stride Counter

Objective: To estimate the number of strides it takes to run to destinations.

Description: Form groups with eight to ten runners in each group. Take turns so everyone within the group receives an opportunity to be a leader. The leader picks an object to run to. The exact distance to the object does not need to be known. Before starting the run, each runner in the group predicts how many strides it will take them individually to run the designated distance to the object. Each runner should count every stride they take as they run to the object. Runners must run in a normal stride length. When all the runners within the group have arrived at the chosen destination, each runner's predicted stride count is compared to their actual stride count to see how close they came to their estimate. Runners are responsible for counting their own strides. Remind the runners that they are on the honor system!

Variations: (1) Run a measured known distance such as 800 meters and count your steps. (2) Run multiple times and tally the total difference at the end to see who was closest to their prediction. (3) Run as a team event with four to five runners in a group and count the total for each team to see which team comes closest to their prediction.

Equipment: Recording sheet

Shipwreck

Objective: To change direction and speed combined with exercises.

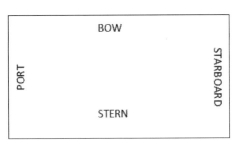

Description: Designate a running area, which will become the deck of a ship. Jog the runners to one side and call it the bow, have the runners jog to the opposite side and call it then the stern. Identify the starboard (right side of ship if facing bow), and port (left side of ship if facing bow). When the coach calls out a side of the ship, the group jogs to that side and performs a designated exercise until the next side is called. For example, when bow is called, the group jogs to the bow and does jumping jacks until the next side is called. The group must keep moving and do the activity called out on command. Other terms you can add are:

Command	Running Action
Fire, Fire, Fire	jogging with knees high, anywhere around the deck
Man the Guns	everyone jogs to the Bow and imitates machine action and noise
Hit the Deck	run to the Stern and do push ups
Take Five	jog the ship, giving each other high fives
Everyone on the Bridge	everyone jogs to the Bow end, huddles, and jumps up and down continuously

Variations: (1) The exercises can be normal circuit training exercises and modified. (2) Change dimensions of the running area and the designated speed at which to move from one area to another area.

Equipment: None needed

Traffic Light Track

Objective: To change the running pace based upon the traffic light colors.

RED   GREEN   YELLOW

Description: The runners jog in a designated area. When the coach holds up a green card, the runners will run fast. When the coach holds up a yellow card, runners will jog and when the red card is held up the runners will walk.

Variations: (1) The coach calls out the color, (2) Form groups with group leaders yelling out a color for their group.

Equipment: Red, yellow and green cards

Red Light/Green Light

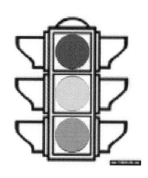

Objective: To move across an area without getting caught and having to start over.

Description: This is a modified version of the old red light/green light game. One person will be the leader and will stand on the goal line facing the opposite direction away from the rest of the runners. The rest of the runners start together and will run toward the goal line. The leader starts clapping. When the leader is clapping, everyone can run. The leader will clap five times and then turn around. The runners will time their running to stop on the fifth clap. If the leader catches anybody running after the fifth clap, they must return to the starting line to start over. The leader turns around and starts clapping again. The runners can start running again when the leader is clapping. Before the leader starts clapping, the leader can turn around and catch someone if they are running. Once the leader starts clapping, five claps must be completed before the leader turns around. The first runner to reach the goal line is the winner. Chose a new leader and play again!

Variations: (1) Use more than five claps for extended running. (2) Use blasts of a whistle.

Equipment: None needed

Tour Bus

Objective: To take turns with a leader being a tour leader of the run.

Description: Form groups with eight runners or less in each group. During the run, the runners will take turn being a tour leader for a designated time or distance. The tour leader will point out sites on the run. For example: "We are now entering the school zone. On your left is the famous Timmerman School. They are known for producing great runners such as me! "After the designated time or distance by the tour leader, someone else becomes the tour guide.

Variations: (1) Runners are assigned a specific route to tour, (2) The tour site is drawn from cards which have a route or map of the route to take, (3) highly conditioned runners can be assigned longer routes.

Equipment: None needed

Chapter 4

Tag Games

Tag is a game that is played worldwide and involves one or more runners chasing other runners in an attempt to "tag" or touch them, usually with their hands. There are many variations on what the tagged runner does after they have been tagged. The goal of the tag games for runners is to keep runners active. Modifications should be made to tag games to keep runners active and remaining in the game. Coaches should modify rules, select appropriate boundaries and equipment, and make sure runners are safe.

Tagging is touching (not pushing, shoving, or pulling) and occurs between the shoulder and hip. Demonstrations of the correct way to tag should be given so that all runners understand how to tag correctly.

TOG (Tagging and Jogging)

Objective: To start behind runners and see how many can be tagged.

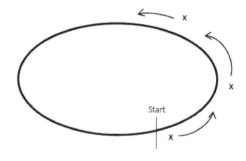

Description: Two or three taggers start behind the rest of the runners on a loop course or track. Vary the distance that the taggers start behind the runners based upon skill level. Highly skilled taggers may start 100 meters behind. All runners (including taggers) are instructed to run counter clockwise. The taggers work to catch up with the rest of the runners. Once a runner is tagged, they move to the outer edges of the circle or track and jog in the opposite direction (clockwise) of the runners who have not been tagged yet. After the tagged runner completes jogging one lap they can re-enter the tag game. Play the game for a designated time period and then switch taggers so everyone eventually has an opportunity to be a tagger.

Variations: (1) Each individual will see how many runners they can pass. There will be no tagging. (2) Form teams and for every runner passed from other teams, one point is earned for the passing team.

Equipment: None needed

Scoring Tag

Objective: To run across a field to a goal line and score without being tagged and repeating the procedure for a designated time period.

Description: Define the boundaries of the playing area with a starting line, a goal line and at least five yards of running space outside each sideline. Form three to four groups with four to twelve runners in each group. Designate one group to be the taggers first and they will stand at mid-field to start round 1. All of the other runners will start at the starting line. On command the runners attempt to run to the goal line without being tagged. If tagged, the tagged runner exits the left boundary sideline and jogs back to the starting line (staying outside the boundary) and immediately start over and try to score again. If runners are not tagged before they cross the goal line they score 1 point and exit the right boundary. They jog back to the starting line down the right boundary sideline and attempt to score again. Each individual keeps track of the points that they score. At the end of the designated time for each round, the runners of each group gather and total their scores. In round two, another group becomes the taggers. Continue the game until each team has had an opportunity to be taggers. Add up the team points from each round to determine which team scored the most points.

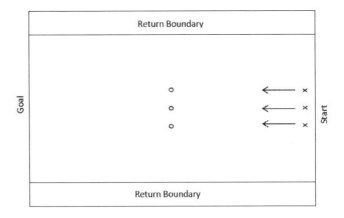

Variation: (1) Add exercises to do once you are tagged and exit the boundary. You must do an exercise outside the boundary line before you can jog back to the starting line and go again.
(2) After an exercise is completed, runners do not have to go back to the start, they may enter wherever they exited the playing field.

Equipment: Cones to mark the boundaries

Note: I often use four groups consisting of freshmen, sophomores, juniors, and seniors and adjust the groups according to size and ability.

Animal Tag

Objective: To work with a group in imitating an animal, while another group guesses which animal is being imitated with the results ending in a chase.

44

Description: Create a playing field with two goal lines and a midline of the playing area. Five feet on each side of the midline, place a run-up line or cone. Divide the team into two groups. Each of the groups will start from their own goal line. The runners in Group A get together and decide what animal they wish to imitate. On command both groups run to their run-up line. Group A will imitate an animal as they run. Group B tries to guess the imitated animal correctly. When both groups arrive at their run-up line, group B must collectively decide on a final answer which is to be given by their designated leader. If the guess is correct, Group B chases Group A back to Group A's goal line, trying to tag as many runners as possible before they reach their goal line. If the guessing team (Group B) can't guess the animal, the performing team (Group A) runs back to their goal line and immediately turns and runs back to the midline imitating the animal again. The guessing team (Group B) also jogs to their goal line and back to the midline to guess again. If the second guess is incorrect, Group A chases Group B towards their starting line trying to tag runners. If the guess is correct, Group B chases Group A. Those caught go to the other group. For round 2, both groups return to their original starting line and Group B now chooses an animal and imitates it while they run to the middle.

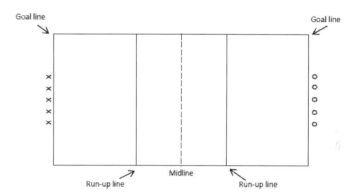

Variations: (1) Limit to tagging only one person during the run backs.

Equipment: Mark two goal lines and two run-up lines.

Rip Off Tag

Objective: To rip off flags of runners and avoid having your flags ripped off.

Description: Designate a playing area. Each runner is given two flags that are attached to the side of the waist of the runner. The goal is for a runner to try to rip off as many flags as they can in a time period. Practice for ten seconds so people know how to rip off tags safely. Do not allow clothing or body parts to be grabbed. A runner can't hold a flag to protect it. A center circle (could be a hula hoop) is designated for the retrieval of flags. After a runner has ripped off two flags, they must take them to the center circle and leave them. Each time a runner has lost both of their flags they go to the center area and do a fitness activity. After the completion of the fitness activity, the runner can attach two new flags and get back into the game. Runners may continue play with one flag.

Variations: (1) Runners can go to the center circle and immediately pick up two flags without doing an exercise.

Equipment: A belt and two flags per runner, a center circle

High Five Tag

Objective: To tag other runners and if tagged, do an exercise before resuming tagging.

Description: Designate a playing area. Everybody is a tagger. If a runner is tagged by someone, the tagged runner performs an exercise such as leg kicks (kicking legs above head). The tagged runner will continue doing the exercise until someone who is not tagged gives a tagged runner a high five. Once the high five is received, they are back in the tag game. If two runners tag each other simultaneously, they are both tagged. Continue play for a designated period of time and then switch the exercise that runners perform when they are tagged.

Variations: (1) You can do a variety of exercises when tagged. Since runners will be giving each other high fives it is best if they remain upright. Some possible exercises to do would be squat thrusts, frog kicks, flex and jump, and trunk twists.

Equipment: None needed

Flip Me The Bird

Objective: To avoid being tagged by having someone flip you the bird (ball in sock).

Description: Designate a playing area. Designate two to six runners as taggers. The taggers may carry a ball to identify themselves. Place a tennis ball in an old tube sock and tie the tube sock. This is the bird. If a runner has possession of the bird they cannot be tagged. Two to six runners that are non-taggers should have a bird. A runner who is about to be tagged can be thrown the bird (flip me the bird) before being tagged. Any runner can handle the bird except for the runners who are taggers. If the runner is tagged before receiving the bird, that runner becomes the new tagger.

Variations: (1) Use balls instead of the bird. If using tennis balls, use a different color ball than what the taggers will carry.

Equipment: Up to six birds (tennis balls in socks)

Powerball Tag

Objective: To see how many runners a tagger (drawn by lottery) can tag in a designated time.

Description: Designate a playing area. Number tennis balls consecutively up to the number of runners you will have. Write the corresponding numbers on pieces of paper and place them into a hat or bowl. Each runner carries a numbered tennis ball and will start running in the designated area. Six Powerball numbers are pulled from the hat. All runners with a ball matching a winning number are taggers. Those who are not taggers drop their ball and run from the winners who keep their ball while running. The taggers try to tag with their ball. If tagged, the tagged runner will do a specified exercise, before they may continue back into play. Each individual keeps track of the number of players they have tagged. Play for one minute. At the end of one minute, blow the whistle or give a command and all non-Powerball winners pick up a new ball. Winners may keep their ball. Everybody starts running in the area again and the coach puts the winning numbers back into the hat and draws another six numbers.

Variations: With a smaller group, you may draw less than six numbers; with larger groups you may want more than six.

Equipment: A tennis ball that has been marked with a unique number for each player.

The Blob

Objective: For one runner (the Blob) to tag runners and have them join the Blob.

Description: Define the playing boundaries. One runner is designated as the Blob. When the Blob tags a runner, the tagged runner joins hands with the Blob and becomes a part of the Blob. Everyone the Blob tags will join hands with the Blob. Only the outside two runners making up the Blob can tag. The last runner caught becomes the next Blob.

Variations: (1) Reduce the size of the playing area as the Blob becomes larger. (2) The Blob can split once it reaches a certain size. (3) The Blob holds a rope and the tagged runners hold onto the rope with the Blob.

Equipment: Cones to mark the running area.

Sharks and Minnows

Objective: To run back and forth across a field without getting tagged and becoming a shark.

Description: Define a playing field with two goal lines, sidelines and a mid-line. Designate one person as a shark, the rest of the runners are minnows. Arrange the minnows in a straight line on the goal line. Their goal is to get to the opposite goal line. The shark will start at the mid-line. The shark attempts to tag as many minnows as possible. Once tagged, a minnow will become a shark. When a minnow reaches the opposite goal line, they turn around and run back to the other goal line trying to avoid being tagged. Continue the game until all minnows have been converted to sharks. The last person to be tagged will be the shark to start the next game.

47

Variations: Play for several rounds, changing the shark each time. Time the game and make the challenge (1) for the shark to complete the shortest game in length of time and (2) the challenge for the minnows to make it the longest game.

Equipment: Cones to mark the field

Capture the Flag

Objective: To bring the flag of the opposing team to your territory without being tagged.

Description: Define a playing area that is split into two halves. Designate a jail area for each half of the field. Divide into two teams of equal numbers, with each team having half of the playing area. Each team has three minutes to hide their flag in their part of the playing area. When the flags are hidden, the teams indicate their flag is hidden and the game begins. Each team starts on their half of the playing field and tries to cross over into the other team's territory and capture their team flag. If a runner is tagged by an opponent in the opponent's territory, the tagged runner has to go to the opponent's jail and can only be freed by being touched by a teammate. The team that captures the flag and brings it back to their half of the field wins.

Variations: (1) This game is great played in the woods, especially at night. (2) Use multiple flags.

Equipment: Two flags

Dragon's Tail

Objective: Two groups form a single file line; grabbing the waist of the person in front of them. The front person tries to catch the tail of the opposing group.

Description: Designate a playing area. Form groups of approximately six runners in each group. Each group lines up in a single file line with runners holding the waist of the runner in front of them. The first runner in line is the head of the dragon and the back runner is the tail of the dragon. A flag is placed in the back pocket of the runner at the end of each line. The object of the game is for the runner at the head of the line to grab the flag from the tail of a dragon in another group. Once a flag has been grabbed, return the flag to that group. Everyone in both groups move up in line with the first runner in line now becoming the tail. Keep track of how many flags your group can grab within a time period.

Variations: (1) To make the game more challenging, make a larger dragon than six runners.

Equipment: Flags

Domino Tag

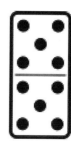

Objective: To tag runners and collect dominoes to see who can get the most points.

Description: Define the playing area boundaries. Every runner draws one domino and places it in their hand. All runners start running in the playing area attempting to tag someone. When tagged, the runner that does the tagging gets to select a domino from the runner that was tagged. A tagged runner cannot immediately tag back. Runners cannot be tagged during the domino exchange with another runner. Runners only have to give up a single domino. Runners can have multiple dominoes but they must be kept in one hand. Runners may continue to play even if they are not holding a domino. Play for two to three minutes and then count the points on each domino.

Variations: (1) Designate ten percent of the group as taggers and they try to collect all the dominoes in two minutes. (2) The tagger selecting a domino can't look at what they are selecting

Equipment: Dominoes

Fox and Geese

Objective: For the fox to chase the geese with runners staying on paths created by circles and lines.

Description: This is an old-time game that works best if ran in the snow where the path is easily recognizable. The deeper the snow, the more challenging this game is. Without snow, you may mark lines with paint or chalk. Cones can also be used to mark an alley. The trail is considered to be two feet wide. Form a large circle and cut the circle into four to eight sections (see below).

The more sections, the easier it is for the runner who is the Fox to tag the Geese. The center spot is called the "hen house". Where the lines touch the outer circle, there should be a hula hoop marking the goose coop. There should be one less goose coop than there are geese. For a group of six for example, there should be four coops and four geese, each goose occupying one coop; one goose is loose on the trail and the fox is in the den in the center of the circle. The object is to run from coop to coop without being caught by the fox. The geese and fox can only run on the trail. The geese can run in any direction, on any line, at any time. When a fox tags a goose, the two exchange places with the fox becoming a goose and the goose becomes a fox. The goose coops are "safe places" and a goose cannot be tagged by a fox while in a coop. A goose must give up the coop if another goose arrives. The geese should be encouraged to run to another coop using a route other than the outer trail.

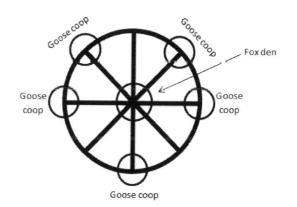

49

Variations: (1) With larger groups play with two foxes. (2) Do abdominal work while in the goose coop.

Equipment: Cones to mark the trails and hula hoops

Exercise Tag

Objective: To tag runners and the tagged runner does a specific exercise associated with the tagger.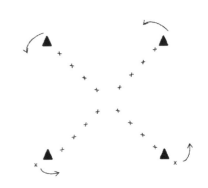

Description: Designate the playing area. Designate four runners as taggers. Each tagger is associated with an exercise. The rest of the runners will run in the designated area. When tagger number one tags someone they will say the name of the exercise and how many repetitions of the exercise they want, "Five push-ups," tagger two, will say, "five sit-ups," tagger three will say, "ten jumps," tagger four will say, "ten jumping jacks." Once the exercise is completed, the tagged person is ready to start running again. Play for a designated time period and then repeat with new taggers.

Variations: (1) The tagged runner goes to the side of the playing area, performs the exercise and then returns to the game. (2) Taggers can vary the exercise and the number of repetitions they call out.

Cone Chase Catch-up Tag

Objective: To run around the cones trying to pass the runner in front of them.

Description: Set up four cones in a square. Form four groups with an equal number in each. Form four lines single file lines with each group. The runner should be behind the cone, with the line extending towards the center of the square. The first runner in each line should be at the cone and everyone else in the group stays inside the cones. The formation will look like the spokes of a wheel. On command, the four lead off runners will run around the cones counter clockwise with a goal of trying to pass a runner. They will continue to run until a runner is passed. Once a runner is passed, that ends that round and the completed runners go to the end of the line inside the cones. The next runners step out and go on command.

Variations (1) Each time a runner passes someone it is a point for that group.

Equipment: Four cones

Circle Tag Slap Back

Objective: To run around or through a circle trying to link with a partner before being tagged.

Description: The team forms a large circle with two runners as partners standing next to each other. This game can be played standing, sitting or lying down on the stomach facing the center. Lying on the stomach is the most hard core, and you will need to warn runners not to hurdle people. One runner is designated as the tagger and another runner is being chased. The person being chased attempts to link up with a pair of two before being tagged. If the runner gets tagged first, then the runner become the tagger and tries to tag the other person back. If the runner is successful in linking up with a pair of runners, the partner on the far side of the linkup is dropped from the link and they become the new runner who is being chased. Runners cannot go back to the original pair or to the pair directly on either side of it. Runners and taggers are allowed to run inside and outside of the circle.

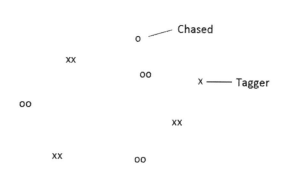

Variations: (1) To make things more interesting, add two or even three sets of taggers.

Equipment: None needed

From Susan Melgares, cross country coach at Manhattan High School, Manhattan, Kansas

Couple Tag

Objective: To tag only your designated partner.

Description: Define the playing boundaries. Runners will partner with another runner of equal ability level. One partner is designated as the beginning tagger. The tagger can tag only their partner. When the partner is tagged, the person tagged spins twice on the spot, becomes the tagger and chases their partner.

Variations: Runners will form pairs with inside hands joined. Two goals lines are established on the opposite sides of an area. One pair will start in the center holding hands and are designated as taggers. On command, the pairs of runners start from one goal line and attempt to run to the other goal line. The taggers try to tag any pair. If a pair is caught they become taggers also. The game continues until all are pairs are tagged. The last pair tagged will be the taggers to start the next game.

Equipment: None needed

Moving Duck Duck Goose

Objective: To tag and chase runners around a circle, while the circle is moving.

Description: Create a large running circle with cones. All runners will be running at the same time around the circle clockwise. Three or four runners are designated as taggers and start running at a faster pace counter-clockwise around the outside of the rest of the runners. As they are passing runners on the running circle, they may tag one of them. The tagged runner moves to the outside of the circle and chases, attempting to re-tag the tagger. The tagged runner makes one complete revolution and gets back in the circle in the same position before the chaser re-tags. If the chaser catches the tagged runner, the tagged runner becomes the chaser. If the chaser does not catch the tagged runner, the chaser goes again.

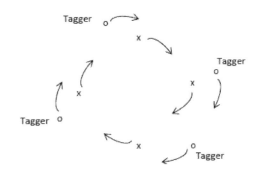

Runners in the circle will communicate to the tagged runner and chaser, pointing out the position they must get back to, to complete one lap. Remember, the runners in the circle continue to jog at all times. If a tagger continues several times, change taggers.

Variations: (1) Drop (not throw) a cloth or a bean bag near a runner's feet to tag them.

Equipment: Bean bags or cloths

Fact or Fiction

Objective: Runners run to amid-line and react to a statement that is fact or fiction by chasing or being chased.

Description: Create two goal lines, a mid-line and two run-up lines, each five feet from the mid-line of the playing area. Divide the team into two groups of equal numbers. Each of the groups will start from their goal line. One team is designated Fact, and the other team, Fiction. On signal, the groups start jogging toward each other to the mid-line. When they arrive at the mid-line they stop and listen to the coach's

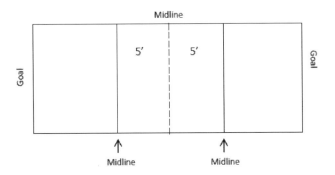

statement. If the statement is false, the False group turns and sprints back to their home base as the Fact team tries to tag them. If the statement is fact, the Fact group chases the False group back to their goal line, attempting to tag them. If a runner is tagged, they become a member of the other group and jog back with the other team to their goal line to start another round.

Variations: (1) You can vary the distance the teams are apart to practice speed work at different distances or change the jogging distance to have a longer active rest periods.

Equipment: Cones to mark the mid-line

Pac Man

Objective: To stay on the lines while playing tag.

Description: This game can be played on gym floor lines or a football field with yard lines and hash marks. Designate three runners to be taggers that will carry a tennis ball to identify them as taggers. The rest of the runners are scattered throughout the playing area and must be on a line at all times. Running can only be on a line. Begin the game by placing the three taggers at the corner of the perimeter lines. When a runner is tagged, they take the ball and become the new tagger. If a runner leaves a line to escape being tagged, that runner is considered as being tagged, and becomes a new tagger. Keep playing until all runners have been tagged. Tag backs are not allowed.

Variations: (1) When a tagger tags a runner, the tagged runner picks up a tennis ball and joins the tagging group. Eventually everyone will be tagged.

Equipment: Area with lines on it, three tennis balls

Chapter 5

Relay Games

A relay can turn tedious running into a game. There are endless varieties of creative, fun relays which can be used to enhance aerobic and anaerobic conditioning. Instead of running relays to see which team comes in first, continue with the relay for a designated time. By repeating the relay, teams can see if they can improve upon their previous performance. The teams do not have to be equal in number or skill in the cooperative style of relay running. Typically the relay baton is a stick like object, but it doesn't always have to be! Relays can be easily done by touching hands, or using objects such as balls that can be carried, kicked, or dribbled. To keep all runners running at once and staying active, use team relays where the entire team runs together performing activities. Relays can create a high level of enthusiasm and energy with an activity.

Balloon Team Relay

Objective: To keep balloons in the air while running.

Description: Designate a starting line and a finish line. Form groups with 4-5 people in a group. Each group lines-up in single file behind the starting line. The first person does not have a balloon, but everyone else should have a balloon. Have the runners blow the balloon up and tie it. Balloons are placed between team members. The object is to have the team members run to the finish line without using their hands to keep the balloon in place. If a team drops a balloon they must stop and put the balloon back in place and continue toward the finish line. If a team touches a balloon with their hands, they must start over. If a balloon is popped they must return to the starting line, blow up a balloon and start over.

Variations: (1) If you are outside, the balloon may pop when it hits the ground. Light balls, such as beach balls could be used.

Equipment: Balloons

Sponge Relay

Objective: To use the sponge as a baton, running with it over your head to cool off with water.

Description: Designate a starting line and a turnaround point. Form two or more groups with an equal number in each group. Each group should form a single file line with the runners behind the starting line. The first runner in each group will have a sponge. Place a bucket full of water at the starting line at the beginning of each line. An empty bucket is placed at the turnaround point for each line. On the command to begin, the first runner places the sponge all the way to the bottom of the water bucket and soaks the sponge. The first runner starts and runs to the bucket turnaround point and squeezes all the water out of the sponge, and returns to the next runner in line and hands them the sponge. The second runner soaks the sponge in the bucket of water, runs to the turnaround point and squeezes out the water in the sponge, into the bucket. The relay continues until a team's bucket is filled to a designated mark.

Variations: (1) The runner carries the sponge over the top of their head. (2) Run for a designated time and see which group has the most water.

Equipment: For each group: a sponge, empty bucket and a bucket full of water.

Pace It My Way

Objective: To learn pace while performing an interval workout with a three person continuous relay.

Description: Run on a track if possible or develop a loop course. Form groups with three runners in each group. The 400 meter track is broken down into the first 200 meters (part 1) and the second 200 meters (part 2). The runners are given a designated time to hit for each part. For example: Runner 1 runs 40 seconds, runner 2 runs 35 seconds, runner 3 runs 30 seconds. Leg 1 and Leg 3 will begin at the starting line and Leg 2 will begin at the 200 meter mark. Runner 1 runs the first 200 meters in the designated leg time of 40 seconds, and hands the baton to Runner 2 who runs the second 200 meters in the designated leg time 35 seconds and hands the baton to Runner 3 who runs 200 meters in designated time of 30 seconds and then hands the baton to Runner 1. The relay continues with runners hitting their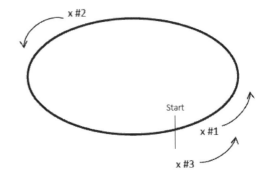
assigned time until a designated distance is achieved. Once a runner completes their running leg, they remain in the same location until the baton comes back around. Determine the total team time. The team that finishes the relay with the most accurate time based on pacing times wins. The coach will need to determine the overall pacing time by adding up the pre-determined individual legs.

Variations: Designate the first 200 meters of the track to be run in a designated time and the second 200 meters of the track to be run in a designated time. The change in pace will allow for runners to feel the difference in pace. For example, the first 200 meters on a track is run in 40 seconds, the second 200 meters of the track in 35 seconds.

Equipment: Stopwatch and recording sheet with pacing times.

56

Circle the Wagons

Objective: To run as a group in a moving circle with one runner in the middle.

Description: Designate a starting line and a turnaround point. Form groups with six to eight runners in a group. Each group forms a circle, with everyone holding hands with the exception of 1 person who stands in the middle of each circle (the wagon master). Each group begins at the starting line, runs around a cone set on the turnaround point and returns back to the starting line. The wagon master in the middle stays in the middle and runs along with their group. When the group returns to the starting line, change the wagon master. The wagon master acts as the driver and directs and encourages the group much as a coxswain would do in rowing. Repeat the run until everyone has had an opportunity to be the wagon master.

Variations: (1) The person in the middle can lead a chant, with the other runners in the group repeating the chant. (2) The driver periodically runs around the wagon to complete a circle around the wagon.

Equipment: One cone (turn around point) for each group

Run and Get Back

Objective: To perform strides in a relay with a controlled recovery by jogging back to the start of the leg when done.

Description: Run on a track or loop course. Form groups of four runners to run a 4 x 100 relay. The runners should take a position on the track spread out 100 meters apart from each other. The first runner runs 100 meters and passes the baton to or touches the hand of the second runner who runs it to the third runner who runs it to the fourth runner who runs it to the finish line. After each individual completes their leg, they turnaround and run in the opposite direction (clockwise) back to their original starting position. The time aspect of the recovery is controlled because the runners must get back to their original position in time for the next baton exchange. This is a continuous relay that can be continued for a designated time or distance.

Variations: (1) Form groups of two runners in each group. The runners take a starting position by standing in the middle of the track on opposite sides of the track. Runner 1 starts the relay and runs 200 meters and then hands off a baton or touches the second runner who takes off running. After completing the first leg, the first runner then cuts across the middle of the infield to get back to the original starting point to take the baton from the second runner. After the second runner completes their leg they cut across the middle of the infield to get back in time to take the handoff. Continue running and cutting across the infield for a designated time or distance.

Equipment: A baton for each team

Skin the Snake

Objective: To have fun doing a teambuilding anaerobic activity by periodically moving a hoop around the group circle.

Description: Designate a playing area. Form groups with four to six runners in each group. Scatter more hula hoops than there are teams throughout the playing field. On the command go, each group runs around in the playing area looking for a hula hoop. When the group comes to a hula hoop, one person picks up the hoop and all the runners in the group join hands and form a circle. The object is to move the hula hoop completely around the circle without letting go of their hands. Once the hoop has made a complete circle they have skinned the snake. The hula hoop is returned to the ground and the group continues to a different hoop. The object is to see how many different hoops a group can get through in a specified amount of time. A group must skin all the hula hoops before they can start repeating hoops.

Variations: (1) To increase running distance, create a home base. After a groups skin a snake, they must return to the home base and touch it before they proceed to skin another snake.

Equipment: Hula Hoops (more than the number of teams)

Race Track

Objective: To combine running a relay and playing tag.

Description: Play on a track if possible or develop a loop course. Divide into an equal number of groups. Each group lines up in a single file line at the starting line. The first runner in each group will run one lap and tag the next runner in their group to start running. Each runner in a group will run a lap. When it becomes the first runner in the group's turn to run again, the teams should be spread out around the track. On their second time running a lap, the first runners try to tag someone running in front of them. When a person is tagged, they cut through the center of the track and go back to their team at the starting line. The tagged teammate's runner in line is watching and when they see their teammate tagged they immediately start to run. A team should always have one runner on the track. Runners cannot slow down and wait to tag someone, and they may get tagged during handoff. If a runner makes it all the way around the track without getting tagged, they touch hands with the next runner in line who starts running.

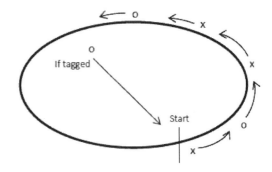

Variations: (1) Instead of tagging a runner, points are scored by passing a runner. Score one point for every runner that is passed.

Equipment: None needed

Donut Race

 **Objective:** To complete running tasks with a hula hoop as a group.

Description: Designate a starting line and a turnaround point. Form groups with an equal number of runners in each group. Groups should line up in single file line at the starting line. Place one cone in front of each group line at the starting line and one cone for the group turnaround point, approximately 100 meters away. Place a hula hoop (donut) for each team somewhere (half-way is preferred) between the cones. On command, each group runs together to their hula hoop (donut) and completes a task such as running through the hoop, jumping over, running around, or stepping in. After completing the task, the group runs the remaining length of the field and circles the turnaround cone. As the group is returning to the starting line, they stop and complete another hula hoop task on the way back. The groups will continue running back and forth for a designated time. To end the game, the coach yells "all in" and all group members must get inside the donut to end the run.

Example:

Sample Activities	
Trip 1	Run through the hoop (team members hold)
Trip 2	Step 1 foot in hoop (hoop remains on ground)
Trip 3	Run completely around hoop (will actually run 1 ½ circles around hoop)
Trip 4	Jump over hoop on ground
Trip 5	Everyone in the hoop to end the game

Variations: Change the activities the runners perform at the hula hoop.

Equipment: Two cones for each group, to mark the start and turnaround points. One hula hoop for each team

All-In

Objective: To have fun and develop teamwork while doing an aerobic activity of periodically placing the entire group in a hula-hoop.

Description: Designate a starting line and a turnaround point. Form groups with six to eight runners in each group. Place one cone in front of each group line at the starting line and one cone in front of each group line, 100 meters away. To start, all group members hold onto a single hula hoop. The runners will run holding the hoop to the turnaround point and back. Runners must have one hand on the hoop at all times. Periodically, the coach yells All-In and all runners must get inside the hoop as quickly as possible with no body parts touching the outside. Once all members of a team are within the hoop, they shout they are done. Score points as the first team in the hoop each time receives one point and first team to finish the race scores three points. The coach should call "All-In" often. The coach should designate a certain number of trips to be made down and back.

Variations: Each time "All-In" is called, the runners must perform an activity such as 5 push-ups, before placing themselves in the middle of the hoop.

Equipment: Cones to mark the course, a hula hoop for each team

Partner Toss Leapfrog Relay

Objective: To throw the ball down the field with a partner, alternating throwing and running past each other.

Description: Designate a starting line and a goal line. Two runners form a group. Each group needs a tennis ball. The two runners will move the ball down the field by passing it. Only the person without the ball may move. From the starting line, Runner 1, without the ball sprints downfield and Runner 2 (with the ball) throws them the ball. When Runner 1 catches the ball they must stop. As soon as Runner 2 throws the ball, Runner 2 starts sprinting ahead of runner 1. Runner 1 will throw Runner 2 the ball. The two runners continue sprinting and passing leapfrogging each other down the field to the goal line. Runners do not have to catch the ball, but can pick it up off the roll.

Variations: (1) Continue back to the starting line and keep repeating down and back for a designated time period. (2) Both runners go back to the starting line and start over if they drop the ball.

Equipment: One tennis ball per two runners

Potato Chip Relay

Objective: To have fun and develop teamwork while doing an aerobic activity of using a potato chip as the baton.

Description: Establish a starting line and a turnaround point. Divide into groups with four to six runners in each group. Each group lines up in single file line at the starting line and is given one potato chip. The object of this activity is for the first runners in each group to run to the turnaround point and back and then hand the potato chip to the next person to run the course. After everyone on the team has run the course compare potato chips to see which team has the least damage to their potato chip.

Variations: (1) Run on a loop course

Equipment: Bag of potato chips

Banana Relay

Objective: To have fun and develop teamwork by running with a banana, passing it among teammates, with the last person in line eating it.

Description: Use a football field if possible. If not, create a field with two goal lines and two end zones. Designate a starting line and a goal line in the end zone. Form groups with six to 10 runners in each group. The runners take their shoes and socks off (a soft running surface is preferred for this activity). Each group lines up with the runners in a single file line behind the first goal line. The first runner will carry a banana. On the command "go", each group runs together to the far end zone and sits down in the end zone, with everyone sitting in a single file line facing the front of the line. The first runner in line puts the banana between their bare feet and rolls over on their back (backwards) toward the next teammate in line while keeping the banana between their feet. The second runner takes the banana with their feet and rolls backwards and passes the banana with their feet to the third runner who receives it with their feet. Continue passing until the banana arrives to the last person in line where it will be started back up the line. The last person in line passes with their feet forward to the next to last person who has rolled backwards to accept the banana with their feet. The banana continues back up the line with runners rolling on their back, getting the banana with their feet and passing it to the runner ahead of them. If a runner drops the banana or touches it with any body part other than their feet, the banana must go back to the previous person who started passing it.

When the banana reaches the front person, everyone on the team stands up and sprints back in single file line to the starting end zone. The group will pass the goal line and turn around to face the direction they just ran from with the group sitting in a single file line in the end zone. The first person in line holds the banana between their feet and the banana is passed from person to person by rolling on their back and accepting and passing with the bare feet as performed earlier. When the banana gets to the end of the line, it is passed back to the front with the feet only. If a runner drops the banana or touches it with any body part other than their feet, the banana must go back to the previous person who started passing it. By this time the banana will be mush!! The front runner has the banana back and is encouraged to peel it and eat it as quickly as possible. The winning group is determined by who can eat the banana and then be the first to whistle out loud.

```
Pass Banana
x x x x   <----------------------------- x x x x
              ------------------------>  x x x x
                                         Pass Banana
```

Variations: (1) Runners leave their shoes on and run to the far end zone. They take their shoes and socks off and pass the banana. They put their shoes back on and run back to the end zone, take their shoes off and pass the banana.

Equipment: One banana for each team, cones to mark starting and turn around line

Note: Pick a person to be the leader of each line that is willing to eat a mushy banana.

61

Progressive Relay

Objective: To progressively add runners running together and then progressively have them drop off.

Description: Designate a starting line and a turnaround point. Form groups with approximately four runners to a group. Runner 1 of each group runs to the turnaround point and back to the starting line. Runner 1 turns around to run back to the turnaround point and is joined by runner 2 as they both run to the turnaround point together and return to the starting line. Both Runners 1 and 2 will turn around at the starting line and continue to run and are joined by Runner 3, as they all go down to the turnaround point and back. Runner number four joins the group on the next down and back. When the entire group has returned to the starting line, runner 1 will drop off and runners 4, 3, and 2 will continue. The next time runner 2 will drop off, then runner 3 and eventually runner 4 will be the last runner to finish the down and back running.

Variations: (1) Run as partners, with two people starting and two people dropping off together

Equipment: Cones to mark starting and turn areas

Rope Relay

Objective: To have fun while choosing rope pieces and adding the lengths of a rope together to see who has the longest rope.

Description: Designate a starting line and a turnaround point. The coach cuts numerous lengths of yarn, string, or rope into various lengths. The string is placed on the turnaround line and is laid out on the ground with one end of the strings covered with a towel to conceal the length of each string. Form teams with an equal number in each group. The first runner for each team starts at the starting line, runs to the turnaround line and picks up a piece of string. When the 1st runner has returned to the starting line, the 2nd runner runs to pick up a piece of string. When the 2nd runner returns to the starting line the 3rd runner will go. Meanwhile, while the runners are running, the non-running group members tie the pieces of string together to form a team string. Continue running for a designated distance or time. The team with the longest string wins.

Variations: (1) To keep everyone running, the entire team runs together at the same time. Everyone on the team takes a piece of string and returns to the starting line. The team ties their string together and everyone holds onto the team string as they run back to pick up more string. Continue running for a designated distance or time. The team with the longest string wins.

Equipment: String or yarn cut up into several different lengths, towel to conceal the length of each stay

Cracker Relay

Objective: To run in a relay, retrieve and eat a cracker, and whistle.

Description: Designate a starting point and a turnaround point. Form relay teams of approximately four runners. Set up an area with crackers at the turnaround point. The first runner on each team will run from the starting line to the turnaround point. At the turnaround point, they will pick up a cracker and run back to the starting line. At the starting line, they will eat the cracker and whistle. After the whistle is completed, the next runner can start. Continue until all members have had an opportunity to run, eat a cracker, and whistle.

Variations: (1) All members of the team will run together. The objective is to have every team member whistle once they get back to the starting line.

Equipment: A box of crackers

Wear the Baton

Objective: To have fun and develop teamwork while doing an aerobic activity of changing clothes instead of handing off the baton.

Description: Designate a loop course. Groups should consist of two runners. The group will decide which runner will go first. The first runner will put on an extra T-shirt. On command, the first runner in each group starts running on the loop course or track. At the end of the lap, they will take off the extra shirt and give it to their partner to put on. Continue the relay using the shirt exchange in lieu of the baton exchange at the end of each lap. Continue for a designated time period or distance.

Variations: The first runner puts on two extra shirts. At the end of end of the first lap, the first runner takes one shirt off and gives it to the second runner. Runner 1 runs another lap and at the end gives a second shirt to the second runner. Runner 2 then starts running with two extra shirts. Continue to run and repeat the shirt exchange for a designated time.

Equipment: Have runners bring an extra shirt or two, preferably a large or extra-large.

H₂0 Relay

Objective: To run and fill up a group gallon jug one cup at a time.

Description: Form groups with two to four runners in each group. Set up three stations in a triangle formation: Station 1 is the starting line. Station 2 consists of a large bucket full of water and station 3 consists of an empty gallon plastic milk jug for each team.

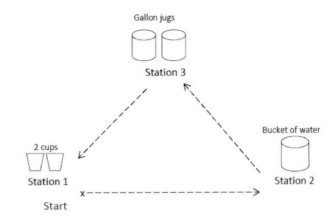

The first runner in line will start with two cups at station 1 and run to station 2 where they will dip the cups into the bucket of water to fill them. After filling the two cups, the runner runs to station 3, and empties the cups of water into the team gallon jug. The first runner continues back to station 1 where they will hand the cups to the second runner. The relay continues until a group fills their gallon jug.

Variations: (1) The entire group runs together at one time and continues to repeat the triangle until their gallon jug is full.

Equipment: Two paper cups (preferably six ounces or less) for every group, a large tub of water and gallon jugs. Each team will need an empty gallon jug. Plastic milk jugs work well. Have team members bring empty ones. Mark the team name on each team jug, or better yet, give the team a couple of minutes to decorate their team jug with colored markers.

Shoe In

Objective: To run together as a relay, discarding shoes and socks and putting them back on.

Description: Designate a running area that runners can run barefoot on. Form groups with six to eight runners in each group. Mark a starting line and a turnaround point. On command, the group will run together from the starting line to the turnaround point. At the turnaround point, runners will take off one shoe and sock and leave it in a group pile. The group will run together and return back to their starting line and take off the other shoe and sock and leave it in a group pile. Now barefoot, the group starts down the field again to the turnaround. Once they arrive at the turnaround point, they put on the shoe and sock they first took off. The group runs together on the return trip to the starting line and puts on their second shoe and sock. Once everyone in the group is shoed, the group runs one final time to the turnaround point (keeping the shoes and socks on this time) and back to end the run.

Variations: (1) At the turnaround point, rather than having a shoe and sock pile for each individual group, there is just one big pile for all groups. The runners take off their shoes and socks and mix them all up in great big pile. (2) Start barefoot with your shoes and socks in a great big team pile at the turnaround point. Everyone starts from the starting line at the same time and runs to the giant shoe pile. Each team member finds their own shoes and socks, put them on and runs back to the starting line.

Equipment: Cones to mark the starting and turn-around points

Paper Airplane Relay

Objective: To see which team can get all of their paper airplanes across the finish line first.

Description: Designate a starting line and a finish line. Form groups with two to four runners in each group. Using notebook paper, each runner creates a paper airplane. The groups will all decorate their paper airplanes the same so each group has an identifiable airplane. The objective is to get all the paper airplanes on your team across the finish line. The groups will all line up on the starting line and on command; everyone will throw their paper airplane toward the finish line and run to retrieve an airplane from their group (it doesn't have to be the one they threw). The groups continue throwing team airplanes to the finish line. First team to get all their paper airplanes across the finish line is the winner.

Variations: (1) Paper airplanes belonging to another team may be picked up and thrown in a direction away from the finish line. (2)Throw the paper airplanes as individuals

Equipment: Notebook paper to make paper airplanes

Run and Throw Biathlon

Objective: To simulate a biathlon competition of running and shooting (throwing).

Description: Form groups with two to four runners in each group. Designate a loop course. At the halfway point and ¾ point on the loop course set up a biathlon shooting station. A shooting station consists of a line such as a jump rope laying on the ground (the firing line), two tennis balls and two empty jugs (a half-gallon or gallon milk jug works well). Set the jugs ten meters from the firing line and set two balls down on the firing line. Set up a penalty area from the starting line to a goal line (cone) 50 meters away and back. On command the first runner in each group, runs to the first shooting station, picks up a ball and lies in a prone position on the firing line and attempts to knock down a jug by throwing the ball at it. There are two balls and two attempts to hit the jug. For every miss there is a 100 meter penalty run at the end. The thrower's teammates will be following the runner and they will work together to reset the station by retrieving the balls and jugs. After the first station the runner runs on to the second shooting station. At the second shooting station, the runner stops at the firing line and throws two balls from a standing position at the jugs. Again, the teammates help reset the station by replacing the balls and setting the jugs up. After the runner has been to both stations they run to the finish line and run their penalty if needed. For every jug missed they have a 100 meter run (down and around a 50 meter cone at the goal line). The next runner in the relay group cannot begin until the penalty run has been completed. Repeat until all runners have gone. First team to finish wins.

Variations: (1) Use four balls and have all the team members go at one time.

Equipment: Jump ropes, tennis balls, empty jugs, and cones

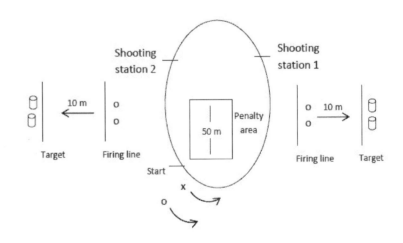

Note: Biathlon combines cross-country skiing with rifle marksmanship and is the most popular winter sport in Europe. Biathletes ski as fast as they can, then they must quickly calm down to hit a target the size of a half-dollar 50 meters away from a prone position and one the size of a coffee cup saucer from a standing position. For every missed target, biathletes must ski a 150-meter penalty loop, costing them valuable time.

Chapter 6

Team Games

Some of the games presented in this chapter are traditional games that have been around for years but are still fun to participate in. Many activities have been adapted from games to incorporate running activities. Throughout the chapter, running has been incorporated into modifying games of baseball, softball, kickball, and golf. The traditional games, the creative games, and the game modifications have been designed to be fun but to also develop the physiological components needed in an endurance athlete. Making running fun is an art. Traditional games can be modified and enhanced, with the variations almost endless.

Circular Attention

Objective: To beat an opponent around a circle and be the first to return to the starting position.

Description: Form two groups with equal numbers in each group. Runners will form a circle facing counterclockwise with one group occupying half of the circle and the other group occupying the other half of the circle. Number the runners in each group consecutively. The coach calls a number. A runner for each group who is that number will immediately run counterclockwise around the circle and back to their original starting place. Whichever runner returns back to their original starting point first scores a point for their group.

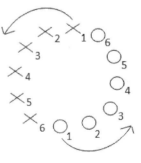

Variations: (1) Call more than one number. (2) For each opponent that is passed, a team scores an additional point.

Equipment: None needed

Cyclone

Objective: To get all of one team's runners back to the original starting position around a circle before the other team.

Description: Mark a running circle with cones. Form two groups with equal numbers in each group. The runners will form a circle on the outside of the cones facing counterclockwise with one group occupying half of the circle and the other group occupying the other half of the circle. The runners of each group are numbered consecutively.

The game starts with all the runners sitting down. At the signal from the coach, the first runner for each group stands up and starts running counter-clockwise around the group. After the first runner passes the second runner, the second runner stands up and begins running. The third runner stands and begins running as soon as the second runner has passed them. Each runner runs around the circle until they arrive back to their original position and sit down. The group getting all their runners back to their original starting place and sitting down first is declared the winner. Continue the game by starting the next round with the #2 runner going first and continue multiple rounds, continuing to start with a different person. Count one point for a team winning the round.

Variation: (1) For every runner that is passed, a group scores one point.

Equipment: Cones to mark the running circle

Card War

Objective: To sprint to the middle of the playing field and see who has the highest card.

Description: Develop a playing field with two starting lines a set distance apart (100 meters) and a mid-line in the middle (challenge spot). Divide into two groups of equal numbers. The two groups line up on opposite starting lines in single file line facing each other. One deck of cards is placed at the front of each group line. The first runner in each group line draws a card without looking at it and sprints to the middle to meet the first runner in the other line. When the runners meet at the challenge spot, they show each other their cards. The higher card is the winner and the winner takes both cards. If there is a tie, the runners keep their card. After showing the cards, both runners run to the end of their line. Captured cards are place on the bottom of the card pile. The next runner in line can start running when the runner preceding them is half-way to the mid-line. Play for a designated amount of time and see which team has the most cards.

x
x
X   Goal line

Variations: (1) Have one line designated as the winning card line. The high card winner will always run to the end of that line. Eventually the winning line will have all the cards.

Mid-line

x   Goal line
x
x

Equipment: Two decks of playing cards

68

Frisbee Softball

Objective: To throw the Frisbee into the playing field and see how many team members can score before the defense throws the Frisbee to everyone on their team.

Description: Set up the playing area similar to a baseball field with four bases. Divide into two groups of equal numbers in each group. The objective is to score as many runs as possible in a set number of innings. One team will be up to bat first and the other will be in the outfield. The batter up throws a Frisbee from home base to anywhere into fair territory and then runs the bases and tags the next team member who runs the bases. The fielding team must retrieve the Frisbee and the Frisbee must be passed to everyone on the team. Note: The outfielders can't run towards the infield until after they have passed the Frisbee. The exception to this is that they may run if chasing a Frisbee thrown to them. Once the runner on the fielding team has caught the Frisbee and thrown it to the next person, they run to the pitching circle (marked by a hula hoop). Once the entire fielding team is in the pitching circle (hula hoop) the runners can no longer score. Count the number of runners that cross the plate as one run each. On a foul throw, the batter loses their turn, with the next person in line throwing. An inning consists of three throws per side and then teams exchange places.

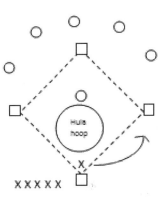

Variations: (1) Once the runner who throws the Frisbee gets to first base then the next runner takes off. (2) Everyone on the team throws once before the side is out.

Equipment: One Frisbee, hula hoop for pitching circle

Aerobic Soccer

Objective: To play a continuous game of soccer with two balls and no goalies that promotes continuous running.

Description: Set up a playing field with four cones for goals. Divide into two teams with an equal number on both teams. Use two soccer balls with no goalies and play does not stop even after goals are made. Adjust the length of the field depending on the number of players. Twenty minutes of aerobic soccer will be about a mile and a half of running.

Variations: (1) Make one ball worth two points and the other only one point. (2) If some people are not getting involved, throw in a third ball.

Equipment: Four cones, two to three balls

69

Fitness Kickball

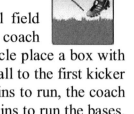

Objective: To continuously kick balls and run around bases before the fielders can return balls back to a box.

Description: Set up a playing area with four bases similar to a baseball field layout. Divide into two teams with an equal number on each team. The coach stands in the pitcher's circle marked by a hula hoop. Next to the pitchers circle place a box with six balls. One team is in the field and the other up to bat. The coach rolls a ball to the first kicker who kicks the ball and runs the bases. Immediately after the first kicker begins to run, the coach takes another ball from the box and rolls it. The second kicker kicks and begins to run the bases. The coach continues to roll and kickers kick, as soon as possible. There will be more than one base runner running at a time. Base runners may not pass each other and may not stop on a base. The fielders retrieve the balls and work together to place them in the box as quickly as possible.

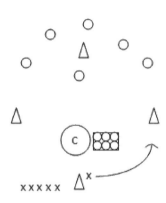

The fielding team must keep the box supplied with balls. If the box becomes empty the batting team gets 3 points. Each kicker receives only one pitch to kick. If the kicker misses, they retrieve the ball and bring it to the box. The fielding team is not penalized for an empty box, if the kicking team has a ball. An inning consists of everyone on the team kicking. As the last kicker comes up, the kicking team calls "last batter." The last batter tries to run all four bases before the fielding team can get all six balls back into the box. When all six balls are in the box the fielding team yells stop and the score is recorded for the kicking team. Play as many innings as desired. The teams have 15 seconds to change sides between innings before the first ball is rolled.

Points	Fitness Kickball Scoring
1	Kicker crosses home plate
3	Every time that there is not at least one ball in the box.
5	Last kicker for crossing home plate before six balls are in box

Variations: (1) A fielder must run the ball and place it into the box; they cannot pass the ball.

Equipment: Six nerf soccer balls, box, cones for bases

Luck of the Draw Strides

Objective: To perform strides based upon cards drawn.

Description: Form groups with four to six runners in a group. Give one deck of cards to each group. Each group member will take a card without looking and then turn the card over. The individual is responsible for remembering the card. Everyone returns their cards to the bottom of the pile. All members of the group will perform the tasks designated on each individual card for their group. When finished with the tasks as a group, everyone in the group draws a new card.

Luck of the Draw Strides Activity	
Ace	sprint full 100 meters
King	build up speed gradually to 100 meters
Queen	build up first 30 meters , run middle 40 meters fast, gradual slow down last 30 meters
Jack	sprint 25 meters, float 25 meters, spring 25 meters, float 25 meters
Joker	jog 100 meters
Odd number	run first 50 meters fast and jog last 50 meters
Even number	jog first 50 meters and run last 50 meters fast

Luck of the Draw Strides Recovery	
Heart	rest 1 minute and run back doing the same thing
Spade	immediately jog back
Diamond	rest 30 seconds and run back doing the same thing
Club	walk back 50 meters and then jog back

Variations: (1) The individual perform the exercise on their card only. (2) Individual runners may take multiple cards at once and complete the tasks that are assigned to them. (3) Individuals take one card for the activity and one card for the recovery.

Equipment: Deck of playing cards

71

Bombs Away

Objective: To retrieve a thrown Frisbee and organize a line around the fielding team.

Description: Form groups with four or five runners in each group. Two groups can compete against each other. One group has a ball or a Frisbee. The first person in line tosses the ball or Frisbee anywhere in the area. The other team will be the fielding team and chases the ball or Frisbee. When the fielding team retrieves the throw, they must get in a straight line behind the person who retrieved it and pass the ball or Frisbee over everyone's head on the retrieving team. The thrower runs around the members of the fielding group, trying to get around as many times as possible. Every time the thrower goes around the group the throwing team gets a point. When the fielding team has finished passing overhead to the last person, they yell stop. As soon as stop is said, the fielding team becomes the throwing team and should throw the ball or Frisbee as quickly as possible. The person with the ball or Frisbee throws it anywhere they wish and the process begins again. Play for a certain amount of time and keep a cumulative total for each team.

Variations: (1) The fielding team passes the ball or Frisbee between their legs. (2)The fielding team alternates passing the ball overhead and between legs.

Equipment: Frisbee or ball for each group

Ultimate Football

Objective: To pass a football downfield from teammate to teammate and across a goal line.

Description: Play on a football field or lay out a similar field. Divide into groups of up to eight people on each team. The object is to pass the football across a goal line. The team in possession attempts to pass to someone on their team. If the ball is caught the person quickly, downs the ball (by touching it to the ground) and passes to someone else. The runners may only take three steps with the ball to stop. If the ball is not caught, the other team retrieves the ball, downs it and passes it in the other direction. No one may guard a person who is downing/passing the ball. After a goal, the ball is brought to mid-field and given to the team that was scored on.

Variations: Play similar to ultimate Frisbee where the football does not need to be downed after every completed pass.

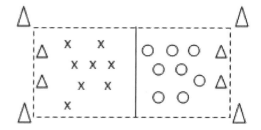

Equipment: Cones to mark boundaries and end zone, football

Soccer Softball

Objective: To score runners around bases before the other team kicks the ball to everyone on their team.

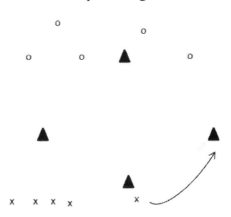

Description: Set up a playing area with four bases similar to a baseball field layout. Divide into two teams with an equal number on each team. One team is at bat. The coach stands in the pitching area marked by a hula hoop and rolls the ball to the first kicker and they kick the ball into the field and begin running the bases. As soon as the kicker at bat crosses first base another runner on the batting team starts at home base and starts to run the bases (without kicking). The offensive runners continue to run the bases as soon as the preceding runner reaches first base. The object is to see how many runners can get all the way around the four bases before all the defensive players have kicked the ball. Once the ball is kicked by the kicking team to the pitching area (marked with a hula hoop), the inning is over. The teams switch positions. Play for a designated number of innings, rotating kickers.

Variations: (1) Play traditional style where only the kicker can run once a ball is kicked. (2) Play community style where the entire team runs when the ball is kicked.

Equipment: Soccer ball, bases, hula hoop

Community Kickball

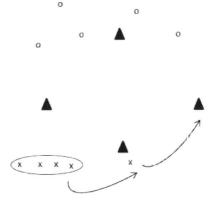

Objective: To run as a team after kicking the ball and get entire team around the bases before recording an out.

Description: Divide into two teams with an equal number on each team. One team will be up and the other team will be in the field. Set up a playing area with four bases similar to a baseball field layout. One team is at bat. Place an empty trash can by the pitching circle (hula hoop). The coach rolls the ball to the first kicker and after the ball is kicked the entire team runs behind the kicker, trying to get around all the bases and touch home plate before the fielding team can get the ball back in the trash can by the pitching circle. The fielding team must stay outside the bases (unless someone has to retrieve the ball inside the bases) and pass the ball from person to person. The defense can't run with the ball. When the last person of the fielding team catches the ball and places it in the trash can, it is an out. There are two methods of counting runs. Either count each runner as they pass over home base or the entire team has to make it around for the one run to count. After three kickers have been up, switch sides. The next inning rotate different kickers, so that everyone has an opportunity to kick.

Variations: (1) If a team is having a hard time scoring, have them talk about a faster way to run, such as running three abreast.(2) A Frisbee could be used instead of a ball.

Equipment: Balls, bases, bucket for balls

Ultimate Frisbee

Objective: To throw a Frisbee from teammate to teammate to cross a goal line.

Description: Establish a playing area with two goal lines and a mid-field line. Divide into two teams with equal numbers. The object of the game is to score goals by throwing a Frisbee to teammates and advance it across the opposing team's goal line. The Frisbee can only be advanced by passing. The runner who catches it is not allowed to take any steps and must throw the Frisbee within three seconds. If the defense intercepts the Frisbee or the offense fails to complete a pass, or the Frisbee goes out of bounds, the opposing team takes over possession of the Frisbee on the spot and can immediately throw to their teammates. Start the game with one team throwing off from mid-field line. The team that gets scored upon will also throw-off from the mid-field line.

Variations: (1) Use multiple Frisbees. (2) To get girls involved, have a rule that a girl must touch the Frisbee before a team can score.

Equipment: Frisbees, cones to mark area

Speedball

Objective: For runners to kick or run the ball down the field for a score.

Description: Establish a playing area with two goal lines. Use cones to set up a soccer goal (six feet wide) and a football end zone on each goal line. Divide into two teams of equal number. The ball is moved down the field by kicking or dribbling as in soccer and by running with it. Runners are not allowed to pick the ball up off the ground with their hands (handball), but it can be flicked up to themselves or someone else with the feet. Once the ball is in a runner's hands they can run with it. If they are tagged, they have three seconds to pass the ball. If the ball goes out of bounds, the opposing team will use either a throw-in or baseball pass. Start the game with one team kicking off from the mid-field line. The team that gets scores upon will also kick-off from the mid-field line.

Scoring: Three points for a soccer goal, two points for a punted field goal if goal posts are available, and one point for a touchdown (pass into the end zone).

Variations: (1) Play with multiple balls depending on the size of the group. (2) Divide into smaller games, using multiple balls (two or three balls). The more balls in a large game, the more the runners are moving and in contact with the ball.

Equipment: Cones to mark area, multiple balls

Musical Running Hoops

Objective: To run until the music ends and find a cone.

Description: Place several hula hoops in a circle. Place cones around the outside of the hoops. There should be one less hoop than the number of runners. Start the music and runners run around the outside of the cones while the music is playing. When the music stops, the runners must place themselves within a hoop. Only one runner is allowed per hoop. The last runner not in a hoop is eliminated, must pick-up the empty hoop, move to the far outside of the cones and run in a counter-clockwise fashion around the cones. Continue to play music and take a hoop out after every round, until everyone but the final person is eliminated.

Variations: (1) Runners play the game with a partner, with two people in a hoop. (2) Use a whistle to signal the runners to run to a hoop.

Equipment: A music player and music

Fear Factor

Objective: To do fun, challenging activities based upon the television show, Fear Factor.

Description: This game is based off of the former television series. The activities can be varied and safety should be a primary factor.

Example Activities:
Activity 1: Draw a line five meters in length. The runners will walk one at a time, blindfolded down the line. For every step off the line they receive one point. Low score wins.

Activity 2: Set up one table a designated distance (30 meters) from the starting line. Set up another table another 30 meters from the first table. On both tables place a bag of candy gummy worms and cups of water. The runners will run to the first table eat a worm and then drink a cup of water. They will run to the second table and eat a worm and drink a cup of water and then run back to the original starting line. The runner must completely drink the water and eat the gummy bear before they can start running again. Time the runners and go for the fastest time.

Activity 3: Obstacle course: An example course could be: Run to pick-up a ball, weave through cones, pick-up a second ball, jump over cones, pick up two more balls and run to the finish line.

Variations: Use your imagination to come up with Fear Factor activities.

Equipment: Tables, water, cups, gummy worms, balls

The Amazing Race

Objective: To receive clues and solve tasks based upon the Amazing Race television show.

Description: This game is based off of the popular television series. The activities can be varied and safety should be a primary factor. Type the clues on paper and leave at the different stations. Although this activity takes some time to set up, the runners love to participate in it. Examples:

Clue 1: IT'S BURIED
On the command "go"- teams travel by foot to the 50 yard line to receive their first clue buried in the trash.

Clue 2: EAT IT UP
Travel by foot to the west press box door. When you arrive at this destination, they will face a roadblock. Roadblock: One team member must eat a worm (gummy worm). After finishing, they will receive the next clue.

Clue 3: FORWARD OR BACKWARDS
Teams must choose to move forward or backwards.
Go to the starting line of the track.
Forward: - Run one lap
Backwards- Walk backwards 100 meters
They will receive the next clue when finished.

Clue 4: RUNNING FARTHER
From the starting line on the southwest corner of the track: The first team member will run to the scoreboard and wait while the second team member runs to the mascot painted on the south side of the field. Once the second runner reaches their destination; they will both turn around and go back to their team. They will they receive the next clue at the starting line.

Clue 5: Travel by holding hands to the 200 meter starting mark and they will encounter a detour.

STACK OR PAY-Stack cones to form a pyramid (3 high). Once pyramid is checked they will get a clue.
Or Pay-One member has to retrieve coins from the bottom of the water bucket. The coins must total to $1. After completing this task, they will receive the next clue.

Clue 6: Roadblock: HOOP IT UP
One team member must hula hoop for 10 seconds

Clue 7: PHOTO FINISH
Travel by foot back to the starting line where all teams will pose for a PHOTO!

Variations: Use your imagination to come up with clues!

Equipment: Gummy worms, stacking cones, coins, hula hoops

Running Baseball

Objective: To play a simulated baseball game based upon the pace that is ran for each interval.

Description: Distribute a score card to each player. Establish time ranges for each type of play with an accompanying point value. Scores are recorded and points tallied to determine winner. An inning consists of 5 minutes. That includes running and recovery. Runners can determine how much recovery time they need.

Example scorecard for a 5:00 minute miler		
400 meter run (1 inning). Every 5 minutes, a new inning starts		
Time	**Play**	**Runs**
1: 08 or under	Home Run	4
1: 09-1: 10	Triple	3
1: 11 - 1: 13	Double	2
1: 14-1: 16	Single	1
1: 16-1: 17	Sacrifice	0
1: 18-1: 19	Strike Out	-1
1: 20-1-21	Double Play	-2
1: 22-or over	Error	-3

Inning	400m time	Points	Total Points/Inn	Cumulative Pts
1	68/72/80	4/2/-2	4	4
2	72/69/79	2/3/-1	4	8
3				
4				
5				
6				
7				
8				
9				
Totals	avg			

Variations: (1) You will need to modify the time ranges and inning length to match the level of your runners.

Running for Par Golf

Objective: To run from hole to hole based upon pace.

Description: Each of the holes on a golf course is assigned a par of 3 to 5 depending on the distance, (3 for shorter, 5 for longer). Every runner runs a test 440 yards at a solid but comfortable effort. Their time for this test run establishes their personal par (running pace par time) for a 440 yard hole. This par pace is then used to determine the proportionate time they must run to achieve par for each different length hole, using the following formula:

Par for hole = Par pace in seconds x (hole length in yards divided by 440 yards)

Calculate par for each hole and fill it in on the score card.
For example: The 440 yard test run is run in 1:15. This gives a personal par of 75 seconds.
For a 300 yard hole, par would be 75 x (300 divided by 440 yards) = 51 seconds
For a 500 yard hole, par would be 75 x (500 divided by 440 yards) = 85 seconds

The scorecard is completed by determining the times for eagles, birdies, bogies, and double bogies by using the following formulas. If the actual running time is between two scores, use the score closest to the running time.

Designate a recovery time to record the scores before the runners are ready for the next hole.

Equipment: Note you can make your own golf course with cones.

	Par 3 hole	Par 4 hole	Par 5 hole
Eagle	Par time minus 6 seconds	Par time minus 8 seconds	Minus 10 seconds
Birdie	Minus 3 seconds	Minus 4 seconds	Minus 5 seconds
Par	Even	Even	Even
Bogie	Plus 3 seconds	Plus 4 seconds	Plus 5 seconds
Double Bogie	Plus 6 seconds	Plus 8	Plus 10 seconds

Scorecard Sample

Hole	Yards	Par	Eagle	Birdie	Par	Bogie	Double Bogie	Your Time	Your Score
1	440	5	65	70	75	80	85	80	6
2	500	4	65	70	85	90	95	65	2
3	300	3	45	48	51	54	60	51	3
4	600	5	92	97	102	107	117	97	4
5	300	3	45	48	51	54	60	60	5
6	400	4	60	64	68	72	80	68	4
7	520	5	79	84	89	94	104	79	3
8	480	4	74	78	82	86	94	86	5
9	280	3	42	45	48	51	57	42	1
		36	597	604	651	688	752	628	33

Blank Scorecard

Hole	Yards	Par	Eagle	Birdie	Par	Bogie	Double Bogie	Your Time	Your Score
1	440	5							
2	500	4							
3	350	3							
4	600	5							
5	300	3							
6	400	4							
7	520	5							
8	480	4							
9	280	3							
		36							

Battle of the Orbs

Objective: To use a variety of balls and try to score by running, kicking, and throwing.

Description: Designate the playing area with two goals (circles approximately 20 feet wide) on opposite ends of the fields. Form two teams with approximately eight on each team. One team will be designated the offense for a determined time period. The offensive team starts from their own goal line with possession of a variety of balls, a football, volleyball, nerf ball, soccer ball, team handball. The object is to move the balls downfield and over the goal line without being tagged or letting the balls touch the ground. If a player is tagged while holding an orb (ball) or if the ball is dropped it must be returned to its origin where the process can begin anew. A player may carry only one ball at a time and it can be passed to a teammate to avoid being tagged while holding the ball. Teammates can be running separate balls simultaneously. The defense will start from the middle of the field. If the ball is run into the goal it counts as two points. If it is thrown in, it counts as one point. The ball must land in the circle before it touches the ground to count as one point. Each team member is responsible for remembering the number of times they scored. When time expires the other team will switch to offense. At the end of each offense-defense switch verify the score.

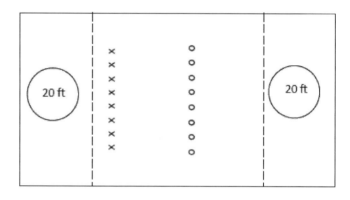

Variations: (1) Add a variety of balls of different shapes. (2) Add more balls. (3) Throw the ball from one teammate to another teammate standing in the opponent's goal to score three points. Roll the ball over the goal area to score one point.

Equipment: A variety of balls.

From Joe Schrag…Hall of Fame Coach from Topeka West, Kansas High School

Donnybrook

Objective: To hit and avoid bit being hit by balls within a circle.

Description: Use the interior of a track if available, if not; use a large rope to form a circle. Form two teams of approximate equal size. Each team will start at opposite ends within the circle with two balls of the same color. The object is to eliminate the opponents by striking them with a ball. Once a player is struck, that player is banished and must move to the exterior of the circle. The banished player is still in the game; however, to retrieve balls thrown by teammates that may go outside the circle boundary. The players still in the interior circle can't leave the circle to retrieve balls. If they do, then they become banished. From the outside, a banished player can throw at the opponent to banish them or throw the ball to a teammate. No blocking of shots is allowed. If a thrown ball hits the ball someone is holding, the person holding the ball is considered banished. The last player remaining in the inner circle represents the winning team. Once banished, a player may re-enter if a teammate gets hit in the head. Only one player may re-enter per head hit.

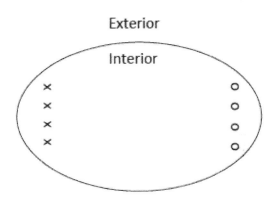

Variations: Use more than two balls (remember they need to be two different colors)

Equipment: Four soft dodge balls (two of one color, two of a different color)

From Joe Schrag…Hall of Fame Coach from Topeka West, Kansas High School

Chapter 7

Fartlek Running Games

Fartlek is a Swedish word that means speed play. As a runner develops high levels of conditioning and experience, they develop the ability to change running speeds. In order for beginning runners to understand the concept of fartlek, structured workouts can be used to guide the runners into changing speeds. Many of the fartlek workouts described are designed to introduce and develop the concept of changing pace. As fartlek training works both the aerobic and anaerobic energy systems in the body it allows for much variety in the workouts. It encourages group running and that makes for more work and more fun! Fartlek workouts can be used for easy workouts or can be very difficult and challenging workouts for the more experienced runner.

Leader of the Pack Fartlek

Objective: To have a leader control the pace and distance for each fartlek surge and recovery.

Description: Form groups of eight runners or less of equal ability in each group. The groups will take turns having a leader, with the leader controlling the pace and distance. For example, runner A will indicate "fast from here to the telephone pole." Runner A leads the surge to the chosen destination. After runner A's surge is over, runner B becomes the leader and dictates the pace and how long the recovery period will be. Runner B initiates the next faster surge by indicating something like "hard from the sign to the intersection." Runner B will control the pace to the next destination. Continue rotating leaders within the group. Give everybody in the group a chance to be a leader.

Variations: (1) The leader does not tell the group how are far they will be running or the destination. (2)The leader can lead for a specified time (i.e. three minutes) or number of surges (i.e. five surges) before the next leader takes over. (3). Combine running with other activities. The leader could include a variety of paces and activities such as: run fast, run slow, walk, complete a 360 degree turn, or do a cartwheel.

Equipment: None needed

Blind Fartlek

Objective: To surge with the leader of a group that has been determined by a secret draw.

Description: Form groups of eight runners or less of equal ability within a group. Everyone in the group is given a secret number. As the group starts running, runners will lead in chronological order of the numbers they have been given. No one knows who the leader will be, then all of a sudden the runner who drew number one starts running fast and everyone else must respond to the pace. The leader determines how far and how fast the surge will be. The runner who drew number two will allow a recovery period of running at a slower pace before surprising the group with a strong surge. Continue until everyone has had a chance to be the leader.

Variations: (1) Draw for numbers to determine what order the runners will lead. (2) A pre-determined distance or time length can be associated with each number. Example: Runner 1 runs three minutes; Runner 2 runs one minute, Runner 3 runs 30 seconds, Runner 4 runs two minutes.

Equipment: None needed

Timed Fartlek

Objective: To run a fartlek surge for a given time and then run a recovery run for a certain time.

Description: Form groups of eight runners or less of equal ability in each group. Each group will run a fast fartlek surge then recover with a slower pace. The time for each surge and recovery is pre-determined by the coach. An example would be to go hard for one minute and then recover for one minute. Repeat for the designated time period. The group attempts to stay together as much as possible. Runners can time themselves or a coach can do the timing.

Variations: Use a ladder format such as: (1) Run one minute hard, then one minute easy, two minutes hard, two minutes easy, three minutes hard and three minutes easy. (2) You can go up the ladder and stop or come back down the ladder doing a 1-2-3-3-2-1. (3) To make the workout harder, run the recovery pace at a steady training pace. (4) In the early season do longer intervals at a slower pace. (5) Shorten the fartlek fast surges and focus on higher intensity.

Equipment: None needed

Indian Style Fartlek

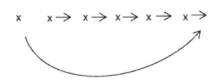

Objective: To run fartlek in single file, with the last runners in the group sprinting to the front.

Description: Form groups of 16 runners or less of equal ability. Runners line up in a single file line and start running forward continuing to stay in single file order. The last person in line will move to the outside of the line and pick up the pace by sprinting to the front of the running line. As soon as the runner assumes the front position, the runner who is now last, moves to the outside and sprints to the front. Continue rotating with the last person in line sprinting up to the front of the line. Run until a designated distance or time is achieved. Emphasize the group staying together (they tend to spread out) in single file line. The total length of the running line should be maintained at approximately 25 meters.

Variations: (1) The group talks to each other, encouraging each other to stay up with the group, speeding up or slowing down the pace, or taking on the hill together.

Equipment: None needed

Team Fartlek

Objective: To run fartlek in single file, with groups sprinting to the front of the running line.

Description: Divide into equal groups of four to six runners in each group. If you have four groups, group A would start in front and run as a pack. Group B runs behind Group A, followed by group C and then group D. Each group should run approximately 10 meters behind the group in front of them. Group D begins the run in the back and on command from someone in group D, group D will run as a pack and sprint to the front and become the new lead group and then settle down into an even pace. Group C then sprints to the front, and when they are in front, group B would then sprint to the front. Continue the rotation where the back group continues to move up to the front. Continue for a designated time period or distance.

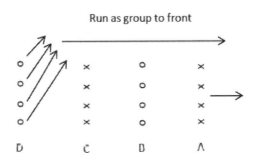

Variations: (1) With two groups, keep alternating the lead with one group leapfrogging the other.

Equipment: None needed

Pick off the Back

Objective: Fun speed play with a focus on surging away and reacting to a surge.

Description: Run on a track or develop a loop course up to 400 meters long. Form groups of six to 10 runners of equal ability. Two runners are designated to be the taggers. One tagger waits at the head of one straightaway and the other tagger waits at the head of the opposite straightaway. The groups will be running a continuous run around the track. The runners in each group pack up as they enter the straightaway. The tagger stands in the tagger circle (hula hoop) until the last person is 10 meters ahead of the tag start line on the straightaway (set up cones to designate the 10 meters from the tagger circle). If you are on a track, you could use the 4x100 meter relay exchange zones as a guide. When the last runner in the group hits the tag start line, the tagger chases the group and attempts to tag someone. The person tagged will become the new tagger and will return to the head of the straightaway to the tagger circle and awaits the next group of runners. If the tagger does not tag someone, they return back to the tagger circle at the beginning of the straightaway and wait for the group to come around again.

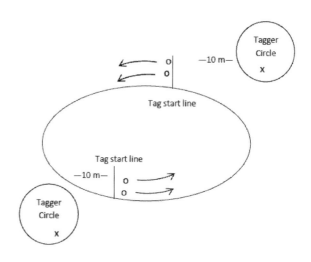

Variations: (1) Rather than tagging someone, the tagger sees how many people they can pass. Keep score and rotate taggers. (2) If the tagger is a fast runner they may be given more than a 10 meter handicap. (3) If the tagger is a slower runner, they can be given less than a 10 meter handicap. Alternate the taggers to give everyone a chance to be a tagger. (4) Leaders can tell the taggers when to start chasing.

Equipment: Cones to mark the 10 meter tagging starting zone.

Lap Elimination

Objective: To stay in the game by avoiding being the last person at the end of each lap.

Description: Set up a loop course (preferably 200-300 meters). Form groups of four to eight runners of equal ability in each group. All runners in a group start together from a common start-finish line. At the end of the first loop, the last runner to cross the finish line is eliminated from the game. Once a runner is out of the game, they must continue running but in the opposite direction around the outside of the loop. The rest of the runners continue running (no stopping). At the end of the second lap, the runner who is last is eliminated. The game continues until all are eliminated except one runner. Smart runners will use strategy. If a runner is a good kicker, they will conserve energy and kick at the end. Non-kickers will have to move earlier in the lap to insure they will not be last person at the end of the lap and be eliminated.

Variations: (1) Once a runner has been eliminated, they can run one lap around the outside of the loop and get back in the game.

Equipment: None needed

Whistle Fartlek

Objective: To vary the running speed based upon a whistle blowing.

Description: Designate a running area. The coach will blow a whistle to signal the runners to begin jogging in a designated area. When the coach blows the whistle once, the runners will jog. The coach will blow the whistle twice for the runners to run fast. Every time the leader blows the whistle once the runners will jog, every time the leader blows the whistle twice the runners will run fast. Continue for a certain time period.

Variations: (1) One whistle equals jog, two whistles equals run fast, three whistles equals sprint, four whistles equals walk

Equipment: Whistle

Number Fartlek

Objective: To have a runner lead when the coach calls their number.

Description: Form groups of eight runners or less. The coach assigns a number and an assigned time to each runner. The group starts running within a designated area. When the coach calls a certain number, the runner who has been assigned that number must lead the fartlek run for the assigned time.

Variations: (1) Use animal names rather than numbers. (2) The coach blows a whistle a certain number of times. The number of whistles will be the number of the runner.

Equipment: None needed

Catch Fartlek

Objective: To simulate a race environment where a runner falls behind and must gradually catch-up.

Description: Form groups of six to ten runners in a group. The runners in each group line up two abreast. They start running forward and on a command or a coach's whistle, the outside two runners split off at a 45 degree angle and continue to run, moving away from the pack. On a return command or whistle, they chase the pack to catch-up. Once they have caught up they become the front two runners in the group line. Repeat as many times as desired.

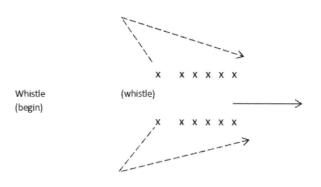

Variations: (1) On the second whistle, as the first group of two is starting returning to the pack, a second group of two splits off. Every time the whistle is blown a group of two runners split off and on the next whistle they will return to catch up to the pack. (2) Develop a loop course or run on the track. Run one loop with everyone in the group together in a pack. When a runners name is called they are to drop out of the pack, stop, count to 10 (or coach can count), and then chase the pack which is continuing to run. The goal is to gradually catch up within one loop. Continue until everyone has had a chance to catch up. The runners should not run all out to catch up! (3) Runners can do an exercise while they are counting.

Equipment: Running area that is wide such as a field or park.

Note: This simulates a race environment where you are gradually trying to get back into the race. It is ideal for a relay simulation when you get the baton behind and you have to gradually gauge your intensity level to catch up, without overextending yourself early. It is also a good simulation for an adverse situation such as falling down or getting tripped. The goal is to gradually get back into the race.

Hole to Hole Fartlek

Objective: To run hard from the tee to the green on a golf or disc golf course.

Description: On a golf or disc golf course, runners will run a fast surge from the tee to the green, then jog to the next tee and run a hard fartlek surge to the next green. Continue in this manner over the entire course or a designated part of it.

Variations: (1) Run a surge from one hole to the next hole, alternating fast and slow. Skip using the tee off area.

Equipment: (1) If you have a suitable area, mark your own golf course by laying out cones for the tees and greens. Mark which cones represent tees and greens by using T1 = Tee 1, G1 = Green 1, etc.

Note: On some golf courses or disc courses, running is not allowed. That seems like a waste of a great running area! Since golfers and disc golfers also like to play on their courses, availability of the course and safety becomes an issue. Make sure you have permission to be on the course. Try to pick a day (such as a bad weather day) that golfers will not be on the course.

Scoring Golf

Objective: To race from tee to green and score points cross country style.

Description: On a golf or disc golf course, the runners race from the tee to the green. The point scoring system for cross country is used with one point for first, two points for second, etc. Each individual keeps track of their points. Walk/jog to the next tee and continue for 9-18 holes.

Variations: (1) Divide into teams and use cumulative team scoring, using cross country scoring. (2) Use individual time and record the times for each hole. Add up all the times at the end. (3) Use team time by adding up all the individual times for each hole.

Equipment: (1) If you have a suitable area, mark your own golf course by laying out cones for the tees and greens. Mark which cones represent tees and greens by using T1 = Tee 1, G1 = Green 1, etc.

Par Golf

Objective: To see who can come closest to their running pace running from hole to hole.

Description: The first time you run this activity, it will be to determine par. After you have determined par, all future runs can use the scoring system. You can set a certain time range for par; a time range for above par and below par for each hole.

On a golf or disc golf course, the runners will run from the tees to the greens. Determine the number of holes you will play. The runners start from the tee and run to the hole. Time each runner from every tee to the hole. This will determine each individual's par. Use the following scoring system once part time has been established.

Par Golf Scoring System		
Time	**Score**	***Points***
time more than 4 seconds faster than par time	eagle	(-2)
less than 4 to 2 seconds faster than par time	birdie	(-1)
less than 2 second faster to less than 2 seconds slower	par	(0)
less than 4 to 2 seconds slower	bogie	(-1)
time more than 4 seconds slower than par time =	eagle	(-2)

Once the scoring system has been developed, the runners run from the tee to the hole. Walk/jog to the next tee and continue for the desired number of holes. Each individual keeps track of their score on each hole.

Suggestion: Give each runner their individualized scorecard so they can quickly determine their points. Use sticky notes for runners to carry with them to mark their score. They can quickly peel the dot off the paper and place on their score for each hole.

HOLE	Score	Par-time	Eagle	Birdie	Par	Bogie	D. Bogie
1		44.0	<40.0	40.1-42.0	42.1-46.0	46-48	>48
2							
3							
4							
5							
6							
7							
8							

Variations: (1) To simplify use a scoring system of below par equals -1 point, par equals 0 points, above par equals 1 point.

Equipment: If you have a suitable area, mark your own golf course by laying out cones for the tees and greens. Mark which cones represent tees and greens by using T1 = Tee 1, G1 = Green 1, etc.

Speedy Disc Golf

Objective: To complete running and throwing a disc over a disc golf course in the shortest time.

Description: Find a disc golf course to do the workout on. Divide into groups with three to four runners in each group. Each group should have one disc. Each member of the group should have a throwing order number. The runner throwing first in the rotation throws toward the disc goal. All team members run to where the disc has been thrown. The runner throwing second in the rotation picks the disc up and throws it to the goal. No running with the disc is allowed. Once the disc is in the goal, the entire group runs to the next tee and the next person in the rotation throws. The purpose is not the least number of throws but who can complete the course the fastest. Spread all the teams out at different holes over the course to start. The teams are responsible for timing themselves. The goal is to have the fastest overall time for the designated number of holes.

Variations: (1) Add a stroke element by adding 10 seconds to the time for every throw that is taken, (2) Participate as individuals instead of groups. An individual throws, retrieves, and continues with his or her own disc. You may wish to number the discs to eliminate confusion. To reduce the risk of getting hit by a disk, limit a playing group to four people and spread out groups to start at different holes over the course. (3) Play for a designated time period and see who can complete the most holes. If you complete 18 holes, start over again.

Equipment: Disc for each team, or a disc for each individual if playing individually. If you have a suitable area, mark your own golf course by laying out cones for the tees and greens. Mark which cones represent tees and greens by using T1 = Tee 1, G1 = Green 1, etc.

Football Lines Touchdown

Objective: To alternate running hard and easy using football field lines.

Description: On a football field have the entire team line up in a single file line. The runners will start on a sideline at the goal line and run fast across the goal line, covering the width of the field. When the runners reach the opposite sideline, they turn and jog down the side line to the five yard line. The runners turn on the five yard line and jog down the five yard line to recover. When the sideline is reached, the runners turn and jog the sideline to the ten yard line, turn and surge hard by running down the ten yard line. Alternate running fast and slow on every five yard line. Runners will run hard on the goal line, 10, 20, 30, 40, and 50 yard lines and run easy to recover on the 5, 15, 25, 35, and 45 yard lines. The runners continue down the field and score a touchdown when they have finish running the opposite goal line from which they started.

Variations: (1) Split into two groups with each group starting on opposite goal lines and opposite sidelines. The groups will pass each other in the middle of the field. See which group can score first. (2) Start as in 1 above and make it friendly with runners giving each other a high five when they meet. (3) Start as in number 1 above. Instead of a fartlek run, run even pace the entire way and race to see which team could have all their runners finish in the opposite end zone first.

Note: I like this workout for early season. It is easy for the coach to be able to supervise and observe by walking down the field.

Equipment: None needed

Back At Ya

Objective: To catch an object and sprint to the front of the fartlek line.

Description: Designate a running loop. Form groups of six to twelve runners in each group. Within each group form a single file line. The first runner in line will have an object such as a tennis ball. To practice the runners will stand in line without running. The first runner flips the ball over his head to the second runner who then flips it over his head to the third. Continue flipping the ball until it reaches the last runner. After the practice session, the group will stay in a single file line as they run and toss the ball over their head. When the last runner in line catches the ball, they sprint to the front with the ball and start the process again. The task is not to drop the object and see how many loops can be done without errors. If the ball is dropped, whoever drops it picks it up and the game is continued.

Variations: (1) Use different objects such as a football or a rubber chicken. To make it very interesting, use water balloons. (2) Toss the ball directly to the last person in line, who will sprint to the front with the ball. (3) If the object is dropped, the group has to start over.

Equipment: Objects for each team such as tennis balls, rubber chickens, or water balloons.

Destroyer

Objective: The leader of the fartlek group tries to get away (destroy) the rest of the group, forcing the other runners to maintain contact.

Description: Form groups of four to six runners of equal ability. Within a group, designate the rotation order in which runners will lead. The goal of the leader is to lead a fartlek surge that is hard. The leader tries to get away (destroy) the group and the group attempts to stay with the leader. Determine a time length that each person will lead. Determine a recovery period that the runners can re-group before the next leader takes over. Rotate leaders so everyone has a turn being the destroyer.

Variations: (1) Leaders may do more than one surge during their time leading. For example, if the leading time is designated at three minutes, the leader may choose to run hard for 90 seconds, easy for 60 seconds and hard for 30 seconds.

Equipment: None needed

Zipper

Objective: To simulate a race environment where a runner falls behind and races back to catch-up.

Description: Form two single file lines. Both lines start running at the same time, in the same direction, staying together. On command or a whistle, the back two runners turn and run in the opposite direction until a command or whistle is blown again. The two runners will turn back around, running in the original direction and try to catch the group as quickly as possible. The objective is to be the first back to the front. When they catch the group they move to the front of the line to be the leaders and settle down into an even pace. Continue for a designated time or distance.

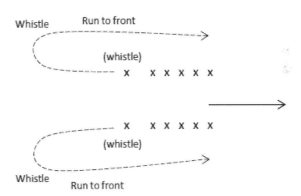

Variations: (1) Once the command is given to turn around and catch the pack, the runners try to catch the pack in a designated time. For example if the designated catch time is 30 seconds, the catching runners will pace themselves and try to catch the group in exactly 30 seconds.

Equipment: None needed

Group Up

Objective: To keep the team close together during a fartlek workout.

Description: Because of varying paces, a group of runners will often get spread out during the workout. This workout helps group the runners up after every surge. The runners will all start together and surge hard for a one minute time period. At the end of the one minute hard surge is a one minute recovery period. During the recovery period, the front runners turn around and jog back towards the slower runner. Everyone should turn around and jog back to the last runner. When the last runner is reached, all runners turn around and run forward in the original running direction. This allows the team to group up during the recovery part and avoids the group being spread out over long distances. Continue the workout using a ladder format of one minute fast, one minute recovery, two minutes fast and two minutes recovery, three minutes fast and three minutes recovery. During each recovery period, the team has an opportunity to group up.

Variations: (1) Continue going up the ladder in distance up to five minutes or more, come down the ladder (three minutes, two minutes, one minute) or simply stop at the top of the ladder. (2) Use any length of workout that is desired, keeping a focus on grouping up after every fast part of the fartlek.

Equipment: None

Russian Tag

Objective: Fun speed play that develops teamwork and both the aerobic and anaerobic systems in a fun tag game.

Description: Form two single file lines. Each runner should be approximately about one arm's length behind the runner in front of them. One runner is designated as the tagger and stands five feet behind the last two runners in the double line. Both lines start running at the same time and run together, maintaining a double line. The taggers run five feet behind the lines. When the tagger shouts "Go," the last runner in each line moves to the outside of their line and sprints to the front of the line. The tagger can choose going to one side or the other and attempts to tag either runner before they get to the front of the lines. Once the two runners meet at the front of the line and touch palms together, they are safe. If the pair is successful in getting to the front of the line and touching palms, the tagger returns to the back of the line to try again. If the tagger is successful in making the tag, the tagged player becomes the new tagger. If the tagger is unsuccessful after three attempts, replace the tagger.

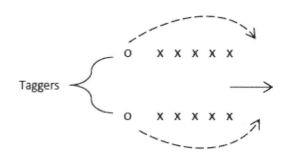

Variations: (1) On the command "Go" the runners being chased move up on the outside of the lines. The tagger runs between the two lines formed by the groups. The objective for the tagger is to high five (tag) a front person in line before the two runners being chased can tag one of the front runners in the line.

Equipment: None needed

Chapter 8

Distance Running Games

The distance run is considered the cornerstone of distance training. Although the distance run is considered a large building block in the running program, many runners especially beginners prefer shorter, fast distances. If endurance levels are low, runners tend to become more uncomfortable as distance increases and enjoyment of the run is lost. As the runner prepares and adapts physically and mentally, the long run become more comfortable and enjoyable. Many distance games can be used to allow runners to physically and mentally enjoy running longer distances.

Formation Run

Objective: To form group formations while running.

Description: Form groups of ten runners or less in each group. Within each group, a leader picks an object that the group will imitate. The group leader coordinates the group into a formation that resembles the object. The group will run in that formation for a designated time period determined by the leader. For example, if the leader says airplane, the group would group into a formation that resembles an airplane. When running, each runner will maintain their position relative to others in order to maintain the airplane formation. Rotate the group leader so everybody has an opportunity to lead. Remember, this is a distance run. The choosing and development of a formation should be done while continuing to run at all times.

Variations: (1) When the run is completed, each group can pick their best formation and show it off in a small running parade.

Equipment: none needed

Flying Geese

Objective: To run together in a V formation like geese flying to achieve a common goal.

Description: If possible, form groups of seven or nine runners. Each group of runners will run in a V formation like flying geese. After a designated time period of running, the front runner drops to the back on the right side of the formation. The next runner on the left side of the formation will move to the lead. After a designated time period, the new lead runner drops to the back on the left side and the next person on the

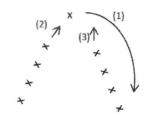

left side of the line moves up. Continue alternating leaders on the right and left side moving up until everyone has had an opportunity to lead.

Variations: (1) The coach blows the whistle for front runners to drop to the back of the formation. (2) Run the flying geese formation as a fast fartlek workout.

Equipment: None needed

Note: Before doing this workout the coach should tell this story of flying geese. Scientists have determined that the V-shaped formation that geese use when migrating serves two important purposes. First, it conserves their energy. Each bird flies slightly above the bird in front of him, resulting in a reduction of wind resistance. The birds take turns being in the front, falling back when they get tired. In this way, the geese can fly for a long time before they must stop for a rest. The second benefit to the V formation is that it is easy to keep track of every bird in the group. Fighter pilots often use this formation for the same reason.

Dog and Cat Game

Objective: To score points by spotting different animals during a distance run.

Description: Before the start of the run, determine a point scoring system of what animals will be used and the number of points for each animal.

Form groups of equal ability for a distance run. On a distance run, as a runner spots an animal, they imitate the sound the animal makes and receive the designated amount of points for that animal. The first person to make the animal sound and then verify by pointing out the animal gets credit for the point. That same animal cannot be used immediately by the other members. However, other members in the group can use a different animal in the herd. For example, if the runners come upon a herd of cows and there are enough cows for everyone, everyone gets one point. If there are only three cows in the herd, then only the first three people to see and make a cow noise would get the point. The game is played until a certain amount of points are earned or to a certain time limit.

Variations: (1) Play individually with each person keeping track of their points. (2) Play as a team with individuals keeping track of their own score and tallying the scores at the end of the run.

Equipment: None needed

Dog and Cat Game Scoring System	
Animal	Points
Dog	1
Cat	1
Horse	2
Cow	2
Pig	3
Sheep	3
Llama	5

Mark My Way

Objective: Allows runners to run on a new course and still find their way back.

Description: Designate the running boundaries. Divide into teams of equal ability. One team (the lead team) gets a five minute head start and can determine where they want to run within the designated boundaries of the run. Every time the lead team makes a turn they must clearly mark it with chalk. The other team or teams are the chasers and take off in pursuit to catch the lead team. When the lead team is caught, everyone jogs back together on the same course. If the lead team is not caught within a designated time period, the lead group turns around and runs the course in the reverse direction to find the chase team. Once together, both teams jog back together. Determine what constitutes a team being caught. It could be the back runner, the majority of runners in the group, or all the runners of the lead group. This run works best if the lead team runs at an easy to moderate pace.

Variations: (1) The girls have one color of chalk and the boys another color. If you have multiple teams use a different colored chalk for each team. (2) Once the lead team is caught, switch the lead team, give the new lead team, a five minute head start and have them mark a different course back to the original starting line. (3) Once the lead team is caught, everyone races back.

Equipment: Chalk spray is the easiest to use, but sidewalk chalk will work.

Camera Run

Objective: To take pictures and document a distance run.

Description: Form groups with two to 10 runners in each group. Designate the running boundaries and a certain time period the runners should be out on the distance run. During the run, the runners within each group document where they go by taking pictures. When all the groups return, each group shares their running show with the other groups.

Variations: (1) Include requirements of what must be included in the picture show. For example the following must be somewhere in the picture: A sports car, an animal, a fire hydrant. (2) The running show could be shared online.

Equipment: Camera

License Plate Game

Objective: To have fun during a distance run by seeing how many different states are represented by license tag plates.

Description: Form groups with four to eight runners in each group. Designate the running boundaries and a certain time period the runners should be out on the distance run. While running, the runners see how many different state plates the group can see while running. Within each group, each individual takes a different state license tag and scores 1 point for each tag. The home state in which one resides cannot be used.

Variations: (1) Use University mascots. Each team gets a University name and mascot and scores one point for every University name or mascot of that University. (2) Before the run, everyone within in each group picks a color. The same color can be chosen by more than one person. During the run, the runners look for their color. Anything that is their color, such as a car, stop sign, or a jacket, counts as one point. The runner has to say that color out loud and where they see it. The first person to use that color gets credit for it. See who can get the most points during the run. (3) Everyone in the group has the same color and see who can see the colored object first. (4) Play with one group against another with each group having a different color.

Equipment: None needed

Twenty Questions

Objective: To have fun while doing a distance run by asking questions to identify a topic.

Description: Form groups with four to eight runners in each group. Designate the running boundaries and a certain time period the runners should be out on the distance run. Determine an order of rotation. On a distance run, the first runner thinks of an object, person, place, or thing that can be related to running. The first question the runners will ask is: "Is it a person, place, or thing? "The runners take turns within the running group asking anything they want as long as the answer can be a "yes" or "no" response. The group continues asking questions to narrow down their ideas until they are able to guess the object. The goal is to see if they can do it in less than 20 questions,

Variations: (1) Limit the topic to running related items. (2) Use non-running related topics.

Equipment: None needed

Sample List of Running Topics for Twenty Questions	
Person	Steve Prefontaine
Person	Usain Bolt
Place	Hayward Field at the University of Oregon
Place	Olympic Stadium- London
Place	State cross country course
Thing	Hill Workout
Thing	Fartlek workout
Thing	League cross country meet

Digital Scavenger Hunt

Objective: To find items on a scavenger hunt by taking digital pictures.

Description: Form groups with four to six runners in each group. Designate the running boundaries. The runners in each group must stay together on the run. Each group has a digital camera or a cell phone camera and a list of things to photograph. Designate a certain time period for groups to take all the pictures on the list and get back. Each team member must take at least one of the pictures. When the runners return, the coach will check to verify that all the items have been photographed. The team that returns first with all the correct items is the winner. If a team does not have all the items, they continue the activity until they have returned with all the items. Place a time limit on the hunt. If the teams have not found all the items, the team with the most items is the winner.

Sample list of items to take pictures of:
Sign with letter "r" in it
Black Dog
Sign that says name of the town
Pine cone
Cow
Tractor (not a riding lawnmower)
Person riding a bike
Two birds in the same picture
Flowers in bloom
Sprinkler watering yard or water running out of hose

Variations: (1) Group members with the exception of the photographer must be in the picture. (2) Add more difficult items to the list and remove the requirement the runners have to stay together and be in the picture. The group will need multiple cameras for this.

Equipment: One digital camera for each team and a list of requirements to fulfill.

Shutter Spot

Objective: To run to a location and take a picture with a group and challenge other groups to guess the spot the picture was taken.

Description: Form groups with four to six runners in each group. Designate the running boundaries. The runners in each group must stay together on the run. Each group has a digital camera or a cell phone camera. Designate a certain time period for groups to take pictures on the list and get back. Each team member must take at least one of the pictures. On the run, the group will take five to ten photographs. At the end of time period, all groups will come together and look at each group's photographs. The challenge is to guess the spot that the photograph was taken.

Variations: (1) Narrow down the number of photos to share with other groups from one to three.

Equipment: Digital camera for each group and paper to write down answers for guesses.

Can I Make A Copy?

Objective: To run to a spot, take a picture and challenge other runners to guess where the picture was taken and run to that spot and make a "copy."

Description: Form groups with four to six runners in each group. Designate the running boundaries. The runners in each group must stay together on the run. Each group has a digital camera or a cell phone camera. Designate a certain time period for groups to take pictures on the list and get back.

On the run the group will take one group photograph and return. At the end of time period, all groups will come together and look at the photographs from every team. The challenge will be for each group to guess where the exact spot that the photograph was taken and then run to that spot and take a picture exactly like the original (make a copy) taken by the other groups. For example, if there are five groups, that means that each group will have to run to the other four spots and take a picture. On command, the groups are off to "make a copy. "Place a time period for the copy process to be accomplished. All groups return and compare their copy to the original photo.

Variation: (1) In the copy process part of the game, each group will only go to one spot to "make a copy," the coach can select who goes where or the groups can, (2) Number the groups and randomly draw to determine which spot they go to "make a copy"

Equipment: Digital camera for each group.

Run and Pose

Objective: To run and pose for a picture and challenge other runners to run to the same spot and pose for a picture.

Description: Form groups with four to six runners in each group. Designate the running boundaries. The runners in each group must stay together on the run.

Each group has a digital camera or a cell phone camera. Designate a certain time period for groups to take pictures and get back. During the run, the group should find a photographic moment and pose for a picture. The runners should have fun with this. The picture should be taken with the automatic feature so that all members of the group are in the photo. When the running time period is over, each team will return and all the groups will share their picture.

The challenge will be for each team to run to the spot where the picture was taken and to pose in the same spot. For example if there are five groups, that means that each group will have to run to the other four spots and "pose" while taking a picture. Place a time period for the run and pose process to be accomplished. At the end of the run, all groups come together and share the posing photos.

Variations: Pose the exact same pose as the group pictures.

Equipment: Digital camera or cell phone with camera

Poker Run

Objective: To collect cards as a team or individuals during a distance run and see who has the best hand.

Description: The course for a poker run can be the cross country course, the track or the sidewalks around the school. Along the course, place stations (checkpoints) where each person is dealt a card from the deck as they run by. At the end of the course, the cards are put together to see which runner has the best hand. Decide whether you will play as a team or as an individual.

Each person is given a sheet with directions to various checkpoints along the distance running route. Everyone starts at the same time. When a runner comes to a checkpoint they are dealt a card to carry the rest of the run. Only one card is dealt at each station. If there is no one to deal the card, the runner must take the first card from the stack of cards that are face down. Make enough stations so that each runner has at least 7 cards so everyone has a chance to finish with a good hand. When the run is finished, see who has the best poker hand.

Variations: (1) The top three finishers that arrive at a station get to discard a card and be dealt a new card to replace an old one. (2) Use Old Maid cards and have several decks spread out at a checkpoint so you can match up cards as you collect them and return with a hand to the finish line. (3) Run in pairs with both runners combining their cards to make the best hand.

Equipment: Several decks of playing cards. You may also use other card games such as Old Maid.

In the event of a tie: highest card wins, and if necessary, the second-highest, third-highest, fourth-highest and smallest card can be used to break the tie.

Poker Hand Ranks

Straight Flush	5♣ 6♣ 7♣ 8♣ 9♣	Five cards in sequence, of the same suit.
Four of a Kind	A♥ A♣ A♠ A♦ 8♣	Four cards of the same rank, and one side card or 'kicker'.
Full House	K♥ K♣ K♠ 10♥ 10♣	Three cards of the same rank, and two cards of a different, matching rank.
Flush	Q♣ 8♣ 6♣ 4♣ 3♣	Five cards of the same suit.
Straight	2♦ 3♣ 4♠ 5♦ 6♣	Five cards in sequence.
Three of a kind	J♣ J♥ J♦ 5♣ 8♦	Three cards of the same rank, and two unrelated side cards.
Two pair	10♦ 10♣ 6♠ 6♣ K♦	Two cards of a matching rank, another two cards of a different matching rank, and one side card.
One pair	A♥ A♣ 8♠ 6♥ 2♦	Two cards of a matching rank, and three unrelated side cards.
High card	K♥ J♠ 10♣ 6♥ 3♦	Any hand that does not qualify under a category listed above.

In the event of a tie: Highest card wins, and if necessary, the second-highest, third-highest, fourth-highest and smallest card can be used to break the tie.

Dice Distance Running

Objective: To break up a distance run into different time periods based upon the roll of dice.

Description: Form groups of two to 10 runners within each group. Designate a total overall time that the runners will run. Roll a pair of dice to see how many minutes the group will run at one time. When the time is up, they return to roll the dice again to determine their next time running time.

Dice Distance Running Example				
Overall Running Time Desired: 30-35 minutes				
	Die 1	Die 2	Minutes Run	Cumulative Time
Roll 1	5	4	9	9
Roll 2	2	3	5	14
Roll 3	1	4	5	19
Roll 4	4	6	10	29
Roll 5	2	3	5	34

On the last roll of the dice, if the runners go over the designated running time, they may stop when they achieve the designated overall time.

Variations: Use this as an anaerobic workout by sprinting from the number of seconds on the dice. (1) Read the low die first. A 1 and 3 would be 13 seconds running time. (2) Use the high die first. If a 1 and 3 were rolled on the dice, that would mean a 31 second run.

Equipment: Dice

Note: Psychologically runners may find the overall running time broken down into manageable sections easier than performing a continuous run.

Distance Bingo

Objective: While completing a distance run, fill out a bingo distance running card.

Description: Divide into groups of 4-6 runners in each group. Each group will have one bingo distance card. As the group is running and they see something on their bingo card, they mark it off. When the group gets a BINGO, they return and draw another bingo card. Play for a designated time period.

Variations: (1) Complete the Bingo cards as individuals. (2) Use different variations of Bingo such as horizontal, vertical, or diagonal.

Equipment: Bingo cards, sticky dots (peel off adhesive backing) to mark bingo cards

Running Bingo Card 1

Pine Tree	White Fence	FREE	Waterfall	Roses
Cross Walk Sign	Circle Driveway	Brick House	American Flag	Tractor
Gas Station	Cat	Newspaper	Trash Can	Two People Walking Together
White Dog	Red Car	Ball	Black Pick-up	Trailer
Speed Limit Sign	Kids Swing Set	House With 3 Car Garage	Woman Walking	Person Riding a Bike

Man Walking	Chain Link Fence	Newspaper	Baby Stroller	Yield Sign
Cross Walk Sign	Circle Driveway	Yellow House	Kansas Flag	Lawnmower
Gas Station	Cat	Free	Black Dog	Two People Walking Together
Dumpster	Blue Car	Person Riding a Motorcycle	White Pick-up	Trailer
Speed Limit Sign	Kids Swing Set	House With 3 Car Garage	Oak Tree	Ball

Oak Tree	White Fence	Speed Limit Sign	Lawnmower	Black Dog
Cross Walk Sign	Blue Car	Brick House	American Flag	Tractor
Two People Walking Together	Cat	Newspaper	Trash Can	Gas Station
White Dog	Red Car	Ball	Black Pick-up	Trailer
FREE	Kids Swing Set	White Pick-up	Man Walking	Person Riding a Motorcycle

Explorer Run

Objective: To explore the area and find answers about different running locations.

Description: Form groups with four to six runners in each group. The runners in each group must stay together on the run. Provide the runners with a list of questions to locations they are to run to as they explore the area. The questions should be answered only by numbers.
Once runners return to the starting area, check their answers.

Explorer Run Sample questions that use locations on your school grounds			Guess	Answer
	1	How many doors are on the middle school building? Count double doors as one.		
	2	What is the largest sign located on the school grounds along 24th Street?		
	3	How many trees are located on the 1 mile loop of the running trail?		
	4	Count trees on both sides near the trail?		
	5	How many tennis courts in the tennis complex are there?		

Variations: (1) If the answers are incorrect they must run back to the locations they missed and check and count again. (2) Have one group of runners run out in advance and prepare the questions and answers to give to the other groups of runners.

Equipment: List of locations to run to

Note: The coach should scout the locations first to formulate the questions and answers.

Stump Jumper Run

Objective: To run to locations marked on a map in the most efficient manner.

Description: Each runner will receive a map of the designated running area with approximately 10 stations marked with an X on the map. Runners will run to each area marked with an X. At each station will be a coded colored marker. Runners mark over the X on their map with the colored marker. There is no prescribed course or order of stations. Runners are instructed to run to each station in the most efficient manner, taking off cross country and jumping any stumps that get in the way (hence the name stump jumper). Safety should be stressed at all times and if the course has any dangerous obstacles these should be pointed out in the directions before the start. When the runner has all the 10 different colored marks on their map they return to the starting line. Once the runners have returned to the starting line, the coach notes their finish time and checks the map for the ten different colored marks. If the runner does not have all 10 marks they are sent back on the course if there is still more time.

Variations: Perform the run in groups with one map per group. (1) Each group will run together. (2) Runners within each group can go to different locations, but must all meet up together at the finish line.

Equipment: Cones as stations, markers at each station, color code, set-up of stations

Note: It is not always the fastest runner who finishes first here. Encourage runners to look at the map before they start running and determine the most efficient distance and route to take. I have found it best to tie the markers down as runners tend to hide the markers from fellow runners.

Clue Run

Objective: To receive clues at different running stations that will lead to the final destination.

Description: Develop a running course and place clues at each station. Form groups with four to six runners in each group. The runners in each group must stay together on the run. The groups will be provided with an initial clue that will lead them to the first station. At the first station will be a clue that leads them to the next station. Runners continue running to each stations and finding a clue and searching for the next station. Eventually, the runners will end up at the ultimate destination.

Clues that can be given that take advantage of locations on your school grounds.	
Clue	**Destination**
Going high, going low, Hanging still when no one's there, Go with the flow, Back and forth as the wind blows your hair.	Swings on the playground
Shoot for the sky, but not too high 10 feet tall, ball and all.	Basketball goal =
Back to nature where the weeds are high, At the head, look down, not towards the sky.	Head of nature trail
Hit a double, don't have to slide, On the ground, you'd tear your hide.	Softball field

Variations: (1) Perform as an individual activity, (2) If the groups are having a difficult time of figuring out the clue, give them some hints.

Equipment: Clues placed at each one of the stations.

Note: I suggest making the clues on a piece of paper. Staple the copies of the clues for each station together and place in a container such as a Ziploc bag or coffee can. Place the clue container where it's visible. Emphasize that runners make take only one clue paper.

Trivia Run

Objective: To solve trivia questions while running from station to station.

Description: Set up a trivia course by placing trivia questions (written on index cards) at different stations. Form groups with four to six runners in each group. The runners in each group must stay together as they run to each trivia station. When the group gets to the trivia station they pick up the question at that station. As they run to the next station, the group should discuss their answer and come to a conclusion. At the end of the trivia run, the runners return to the starting area, to check their answers with the coach. For each number that they are off from the correct answer they will do that many repetitions of a particular exercise.

Example questions and exercises:

	Sample Questions	Exercise	Guess	Answer	Reps
Running Trivia					
1	How many runners officially make up a full cross country team?	Laps around lower pond			
2	How many runners for each team score points toward the team score?	Laps around upper pond			
3	How many hills are on our home cross country course?	40 yard sprints			
4	How many girls are on our cross country team?	Sprints to flagpole			
5	How many boys are on our cross country team?	Sprints to flagpole			
6	Average age of girls cross country team?	30 second runs per month off			
7	How far do the girls run at state cross country meet?	10 minute runs			
8	Average age of boys cross country team?	30 second run per month off			
9	How many ditches are on the cross country course?	40 yard skips			
10	How many toilet seats are available in the restroom on our cross country course?	100 meter Strides			
Bonus	Who is better looking; the boys' XC team or girls' XC team?	Laps around the city limits			

	Question	Exercise	Guess	Answer	Reps
Sample: Running Trivia					
1	How many runners officially make up a full cross country team?	Laps around lower pond	7	7	0
2	How many runners for each team score points toward the team score?	Laps around upper pond	7	5	2
3	How many hills are on our home cross country course?	40 yard sprints	11	7	4
4	How many girls are on our cross country team?	Sprints to flagpole	23	25	2
5	How many boys are on our cross country team?	Sprints to flagpole	31	24	7
6	Average age of girls cross country team?	30 second runs per month off	15.7	16.2	2.5
7	How far do the girls run at state cross country meet?	10 minute runs	4K	4K	0
8	Average age of boys cross country team?	30 second run per month off	16.0	17.0	1
9	How many ditches are on the cross country course?	40 yard skips	3	5	2
10	How many toilet seats are available in the restroom on our cross country course?	100 meter Strides	6	2	4
Bonus	Who is better looking; the boys' XC team or girls' XC team?	Laps around the city limits	?	?	?

Variations: (1) Run as individuals. (2) Run the entire team over the course, stopping at each station to complete the trivia question and the exercise before going on to the next station. One possibility is to have a boys group and a girls group competing against each other. (3) Talk about the tradition of your program as you go over the course.

Equipment: Trivia questions on index cards

Note: On our home cross country course we have certain parts of the course named after our school team and individual state cross country champions. Before our first home meet, we will run over the course and play championship trivia. This is an excellent and fun way to educate the team about the school tradition as well as familiarize them with the course.

Stagger Run

Objective: To challenge faster runners by having them start behind slower runners on a distance run.

Description: Designate a running distance. Use a handicap system where the slower runners will start ahead of the faster runners. If the handicap is accurate all runners will theoretically finish at the exact time. The difficulty lies in estimating the correct handicap. Several methods to achieve this are discussed in the variations section.

Variations: (1) If the distance chosen to run is the same as a previous race, use the time differences in the previous race. (2) If the distance chosen to run is a different distance that any previous race, use the previous race pace. (3) Use an age system. (4) Use a class system such as freshman, sophomore, and junior, senior with the younger runners receiving a bigger handicap.

Equipment: None needed

Note: This is an excellent way to challenge faster runners to chase runners that are allowed to start ahead of them.

Meet in the Middle Run

Objective: An aerobic activity that uses teamwork and allows better runners to run farther.

Description: Designate a loop course. Runners form groups of two. From a common start-finish line, each member of the group runs in an opposite direction on the loop course. When they meet running towards each other on the course, they high five each other and turn around and run back in the direction they came from. When they have both arrived back at the start-finish line, they high five each other and their team has finished. Try to pair the teams up so they are even. For example, place the fastest runner with your slowest runner, next fastest with next slowest. This workout will have both runners running the same amount of time, but will allow your faster runners to run farther and the slower runners will run less.

Variations: (1) Keep score after each round, using cross country scoring with the winning team receiving one point, second place two points, etc. (2) Make this a continuous run. When a team has finished one loop, they high five and immediately start over. (3) Add an exercise to do when both runners meet in the middle.

Equipment: Cones to mark loop

Chapter 9

Specific Training Running Games

The principle of specificity states to become good at something, do that thing. To race at a high level, runners need to simulate that high level of racing in training as closely as possible. Every type of run (fartlek, long, easy, tempo, intervals) serves different purposes. Each type of run stresses different systems within the body and continued exposure to the specific workouts develops specific physiological adaptations. The running games in this chapter are designed for the more competitive runner who wishes to focus on specific, more difficult workouts to be able to race at a higher performance level.

Predict Runs

Objective: To see who comes closest to their predicted time.

Description: Designate a location to run to and back. This is not a race to see who is the fastest; the goal is to see who comes closest to their predicted time. Collect all watches before the start of the run. A recorder writes down what each runner predicts they will run for the out and back course, on a recording sheet. On command, all runners run to the designated location and back. The coach reads the time as runners return. Runners must maintain their pace as they near the finish. Do not allow them to adjust their pace as they hear the time. Runners are responsible for remembering their time as they finish and how far off their predicted time they were. The person closest to their predicted time is the winner. Pick various locations to run to (it is not important to know the distance).

Variations: (1) Form groups with all members of the group starting together and every group member must finish before the time ends. The group closest to their predicted time is the winner. (2) Add the times each individual is off to get a total group time. (3) Run several rounds and score as a cross country meet. The closest to the predicted time receives one point, the second closest two points, etc.

Equipment: Stopwatch, recording sheet

Road Rally

Objective: For teams to learn how to run at a designated pace.

Description: Form groups of six to eight in each group. Let each group name themselves after a car. Give each group a stopwatch and a road rally card to record its time for each station. A designated pace will be written on the road rally card. All members of the group complete the station attempting to run the designated pace. Each group is responsible for recording their own time. The team then will proceed to next activity, check the distance and pace start the watch and begin the activity. The team closest to actual time is the winner. The coach has the key listing the correct time for each station. Once a group has completed the stations they check with the coach to receive the pace key and then calculate the time they were off on each station. Each group then determines the total time off and the group closest to the pace (least time off) is the winning group.

Short Course

Station	Distance	Pace	Actual Time	Correct Time	Time off
Station 1	Run 220 yards	8 mph			
Station 2	Run 110 yards	10 mph			
Station 3	Walk 440 yards	3.5 mph			
Station 4	Run 400 yards	7.5 mph			
Station 5	Walk backwards 100 yards	3.0 mph			
Station 6	Run 440 yards	7.5 mph			
Total					

Short Course Key

Station	Distance	Pace	Actual Time	Correct Time	Time off
Station 1	Run 220 yards	8 mph		56.27	
Station 2	Run 110 yards	10 mph		22.49	
Station 3	Walk 440 yards	3.5 mph		4:17.4	
Station 4	Run 400 yards	7.5 mph		1:48.6	
Station 5	Walk backwards 100 yards	3.0 mph		1:08.18	
Station 6	Run 440 yards	7.5 mph		2:00	
Total				10:32.94	

Long Course

Station	Distance	Pace	Actual Time	Correct Time	Time Off
Station 1	Run 1 mile	7 mph			
Station 2	Walk 440 yards	3.5 mph			
Station 3	Run ½ mile	8 mph			
Station 4	Run ¾ mile	7.5 mph			
Station 5	Jog 440 yards	6 mph			
Station 6	Run 1 mile	7 mph			
Total					

Long Course Key

Station	Distance	Pace	Actual Time	Correct Time	Time Off
Station 1	Run 1 mile	7 mph		8:51.6	
Station 2	Walk 440 yards	3.5 mph		4:17.4	
Station 3	Run ½ mi	8 mph		3:45	
Station 4	Run ¾ mi	7.5 mph		6:00	
Station 5	Jog 440 yards	6 mph		2:30	
Station 6	Run 1 mile	7 mph		8:34.2	
Total				33:58.2	

Variations: (1). The above paces were calculated using yards and miles per hour. You could use meters and meters per second. (2) Distances and times can be varied according to ability.

Equipment: Cones to mark each station
A road rally recording sheet, pencil and stopwatch for each group
A key card for coach showing correct times the runner should hit for each station.

Note: The runners are given a speed in miles per hour, not a set time for each station. The challenge is to determine the correct pace to run. The distances given are in yards to match miles per hour.

Out and Back Pacer

Objective: To run the same pace on a course going out and coming back.

Description: The coach or the runners select a destination to run towards. Runners are not allowed to wear watches. Each runner should have a pre-determined pace, either self-determined or coach assigned. On command, the runners start running at their individually determined pace. After a time

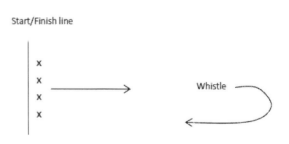

period determined by the coach, the coach blows the whistle and all runners will stop where they are. The coach notes the running time. After a brief recovery period, the whistle is blown again and runners attempt to run back to the starting point at the exact same pace. The whistle is blown again when the time matches the first run. The runner closest to the start/finish line wins. Give points similar to cross country where the winner gets one point, second place gets two points, etc. Perform the activity for a series of runs and tally the points. Low score wins! The runners must keep their pace and can't stop or slow as they approach the finish line. Some runners may have to continue running past the finish line.

Variations: (1) If runners slow down as they near the finish line so they don't go over the line, penalize them with a point. (2) Determine a winner by using the distance each runner is from the start/finish line, measured by having the runner step it off.

Equipment: Stopwatch, whistle

Make it- Take it Intervals

Objective: To lead an interval group and achieve the designated pace time to keep on leading the intervals.

Description: Form groups of four to six runners of equal ability in each group. The coach designates a certain time the group should hit for the interval workout. Runner 1 leads the first interval. If Runner 1 is within + or – half a second of the assigned interval time (make it) they remain the leader (take it) for the next interval. Runner 1 will continue being the leader until they do not make the designated time. When Runner 1 does not make the designated time, a new leader will take over. Continue until you have run the desired number of intervals.

Variation: (1) Score the intervals; each time the runner makes the time, they receive one point.

Equipment: Stopwatch

Last Man Counts

Objective: For a team to achieve a predicted time by working together to help the last runner run faster.

Description: Form groups with approximately five runners in each group. The coach determines a distance to be run and a time for each group. The official time for the group will be based on the last runner (fifth man). It is important that the top four runners encourage the last runner, because their team time depends on the fifth runner. Run several intervals and record the times and how far off the determined time the group is.

Variations: (1) Base the winning group on who was the most accurate in achieving their designated time. (2) Add the times at the end of the workout with the fastest group winning. (3) Take the time difference between the first person in the group and the last person in the group. Keep track of the total time distance, with low time winning.

Equipment: Recording sheet, stopwatch

Hill Tag

Objective: To have fun playing tag and at the same time practice running uphill.

Description: This workout works best with a playing field that is uphill such as in a park. The area does not have to be completely open and can contain trees. Form three to four groups with four to 12 runners in each group. Designate a starting line at the bottom of the hill and a goal line at the top of the hill. Also designate the side boundaries. Designate one group to be the taggers first and they will start at the goal line (top of the hill). All of the other runners will start at the starting line (bottom of the hill) and attempt to run to the goal line without being tagged. Runners can avoid being tagged if they take at least three steps downhill (but remember the goal is to run uphill.) If tagged, the runner runs back to the starting line, by running down the sideline, starts from the starting line again and tries to score. If runners are not tagged before they cross the goal line they score one point and run down the side boundary to return to the starting line and attempt to score again. Each individual keeps track of the points that they score. At the end of the designated time, the runners of each group gather and total their scores. In round two, another group becomes the taggers. Continue the game until each group has had an opportunity to be taggers. Add up the points from each round to determine which group scored the most points.

Variations: (1) Runners must run to the sideline and perform an exercise after being tagged. (2) Runners do not have to go back to the start; they may begin going uphill again after performing an exercise.

Equipment: Cones to mark the boundaries

Gut Buster

Objective: To maintain contact while running a fast pace being paced by a bike.

Description: Form groups of equal ability. This workout is best done on the roads. You will need one bike per group. After a sufficient warm-up period, the person riding the bike in each group will set a very strong pace for the runners. The pace set by the bike should pose a strong challenge for the runners to keep up. Once a runner in the group cannot keep up the pace and loses contact by dropping ten meters or more behind the pack, they are eliminated from the Gut

Buster. After elimination, runners continue to jog in the same direction. The bike continues pacing until the last runner cannot hold the pace. For recovery, the bike and the last runner turns around and heads back in the opposite direction picking up runners until the group is all back together again. Rotate by placing a different person on the bike for each Gut Buster surge.

Variations: (1) The coach rides the bike. (2) An injured runner rides the bike. This serves a dual purpose of the injured runner receiving a cardiovascular workout and still feeling like they are a contributing member of the team.

Equipment: One bike for each group

Pursuit

Objective: To catch a runner a half a lap ahead.

Description: Run on a track or designate a loop course. Form groups with two runners in a group of equal ability. The two runners start on opposite sides from each other in the middle of the track. The goal is to run around the loop and catch the other runner. Coaches may set a certain time period to run for. The contest ends when one runner catches the other or the time period is reached. At the end of the time period see which runner has run the furthest.

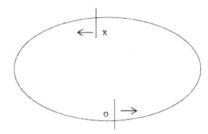

Variation: (1) Run for a designated distance or time. If one runner passes another the game does not end, but continues to run for the designated distance or time. (2) Shorten the loop so it will be easier to catch someone. (3) Form groups of a fast runner and a slower runner. The goal of the fast runner is to catch the slow runner. The goal of the slow runner is not to get caught. Play for a designated time period.

Equipment: None needed

Note: This is similar to a bike pursuit race in which the two riders start on opposite sides of the track and chase each other.

Team Pursuit

Objective: To work as a team to catch a team a half a lap ahead.

Description: Form teams with four runners of equal ability on each team. Two teams start on opposite sides from each other in the middle of the track. The goal is

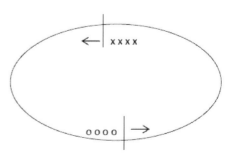

to run around the loop and catch the other team. Coaches may set a certain time period to run for. Each team must alternate leaders every lap. The contest ends when one team catches the other or the time period is reached. At the end of the time period see which team has run the furthest. Catching the other team is defined as the last runner on the team passes one runner on the other team. This is similar to a team bike pursuit race.

Variations: (1) Run for a designated distance. If one team passes another continue to run for the designated distance. (2) Shorten the loop so it will be easier to catch someone. (3) Form groups of a fast team and a slow team. The goal of the fast team is to catch the slow team. The goal of the slow team is not to get caught within a designated time period.

Equipment: None needed

The Breakaway

Objective: To work on breaking away and catching up to runners.

Description: Divide into groups of equal ability. Number each group. All groups start out running a steady pace together. Group 1 will start a breakaway by surging hard and the other teams will continue running a steady pace. After a designated time (30 seconds), the breakaway group settles back into a steady pace and the remaining groups (pursuit groups) push the pace to catch up to the breakaway group. Once the breakaway group is caught, group 2 becomes the breakaway group. Continue until each group has had a chance to be the breakaway group. Each group should alternate group leaders in catching up.

Variations: (1) Periodically someone may yell "break it." This is the signal for all teams to pick up the pace. The goal is for a team to get all their runners ahead of the other teams and run ahead of them for 30 seconds. The runners within a team must stay together. Runners should encourage back of the pack runners to keep up!

Equipment: None needed

Team Bridge

Objective: To work with a group to gradually move up from one group of runners to another group.

Description: Divide into four groups with runners of equal ability. Groups 1, 2, and 3 are given a pre-determined pace to run. Group 4 will start as the chase group. Group 1 starts with a three minute head start, group 2 starts with a two minute head start, and group 1 starts with a one minute head start. Group 4 (chase group) is trying to bridge the gap between groups and

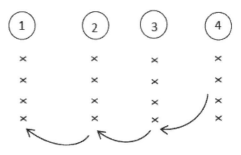

119

will run hard until they catch group 3. After catching up with group 3, they run with them for one minute before picking up the pace to catch (bridge) group 2. After catching group 2 and running with them for one minute, they bridge up to group 1. This ends round one and everybody groups up for a recovery run. For the second round, group 4 will be the first group starting with a three minute head start, group 3 will have a two minute head start and group 2 will have a one minute head start. Group 1 will become the chase group. Keep alternating on each round so that every team has a run at each of the starting and chasing positions.

Variations: (1) Alternate leaders within each group. (2)Run with a group for more than one minute

Equipment: None needed

Individual Bridge

Objective: To work as an individual to gradually move up from one group of runners to another group.

Description: Divide into four groups with runner of equal ability. Within each group, every runner should have an assigned a number. Groups 1, 2, and 3 are given a pre-determined pace to run. Group 4 will be the chase group. Group 1 starts with a three minute head start, group 2 starts with a two minute head start, and group 1 starts with a one minute head start. Runners in group 4 are trying to bridge the gap between groups and will run hard until they catch group 3. Runners in group 4 (chase group) will leave their group one runner at a time in one minute intervals starting with runner 1. After each individual catches group 3, they run with them for two minutes. Then individually they pick up the pace to catch (bridge) group 2. After catching them and running with them for two minutes, they bridge up to group 1. When a chase person joins group 1, (the front group) one person from group 1 jogs slowly until they are in the last group. Every time a runner catches up to group one, a member of group 1 slows down and drops to the back to the last group. This continues until everyone in group 4 has had the opportunity to bridge the gap and have now become group 1. Group 4 has now become the lead group. Repeat the chasing sequence and when everyone in the chase group has moved up to the front group, round one has ended. For the second round, group 2 and 3 will switch places with 1 and 4 and go again. This will allow everyone to be a chaser.

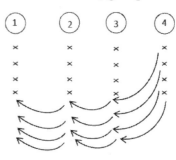

Variation: Relay Bridge: Run relay style. Each group has a runner in pack 1, 2, 3, 4. When the first runner reaches the second runner in pack 2, the second runner picks up the pace to catch pack 3. When the second runner catches pack 3, the third runner picks it up to catch pack 4. When they catch pack 4, the fourth runner jogs back to pack 1and it begins again.

Equipment: None needed

Running Tournament (Track Madness)

Objective: To run an interval workout and work on pace in a fun manner.

Description: Form groups of up to eight runners. Set up a tournament bracket. Each of the eight runners in a group will draw to see where the runner goes in the bracket. Instead of a winners and losers bracket call it an advance and retreat bracket. Once the runner's name has been placed in the bracket, each runner should determine or be given a pace to hit. The pace should be individualized for each runner and does not have to be the same pace for everyone in the group. The two runners on the same side of the bracket will run against each other and the one closest to their correct pace advances on to the next round. Determine the distance to be run and what the recovery interval will be. The coach reads the time as the runners cross the finish line. Runners should be warned not to adjust their pace if they hear the time before they cross the finish line. Runners determine how far off they were on their pace and go over to the tournament bracket and write their time down by their name in the bracket. After both runners that ran against each other have recorded their times, determine who advances or retreats in the bracket. Everyone runs three rounds to determine the champion and the final places. After a recovery period, redraw positions for a new bracket and a new set of intervals.

Variations: Instead of pace, go off of whoever runs the fastest. You may want to seed the tournament instead of drawing by lot. Encourage the runners to pace themselves as they will be running multiple runs throughout the tournament.

5-8 Person Bracket- (run sets of three intervals)

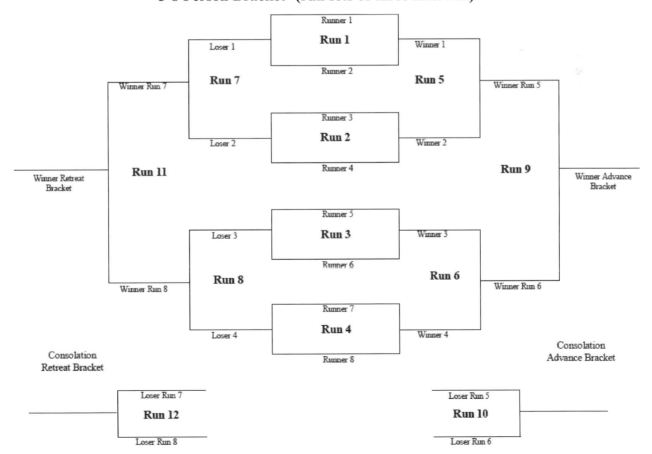

1-4 person bracket (run sets of two intervals)

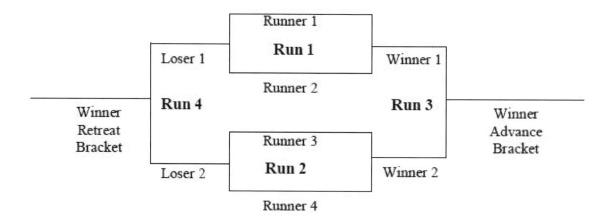

Climb the Pace Challenge Ladder

Objective: To challenge a teammate of running pace, with the most accurate runner moving higher on the ladder.

Description: The runners should determine or be given a pace to hit for one interval run. Everybody runs one interval run and a pace challenge ladder is formed in the order of closest to farthest away from the pace they were to hit. Each runner should print their name on an index card and place it on the ground or a board in the order of the pace challenge ladder. Determine how many intervals will be done and the recovery interval between each one. A runner may challenge someone within four spots of them on the ladder. The goal is to see who comes closest to their pace. The person that is the closest to their pace takes the higher spot held between the two runners and the person farthest away from the predicted pace takes the lower spot.

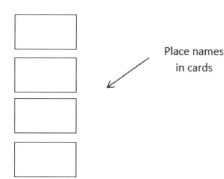

Place names in cards

Variations: (1) Instead of pace go off of whoever runs the fastest. The first run determines the place on the challenge ladder. Encourage the runners to pace themselves as they will be running multiple runs.

Equipment: Stopwatches, no watches are allowed when running

R-U-N (Running version of Basketball HORSE game)

Objective: To challenge teammates in a running task (similar to a basketball game of HORSE).

Description: Form groups with three or four runners of equal ability in each group. Establish a numerical order in the group. Runner number 1 will issue a challenge to the other runners in their group. For example: "Run 100 meters in 16 to 17seconds." Runner number 1 then takes the challenge and attempts to run 100 meters in 16 to 17seconds. The other members of the group will time the partner and run behind them. If runner 1 achieves their stated goal, the other runner in the group must match the challenge. Runner 1 will time the other runners in the group and run behind them as they take the challenge. If the challenge is not met, the other runners receive the letter R. If runner 1 does not achieve what they stated the other runners do not have to attempt to match it and it becomes Runner number 2's turn. Runner number 2 is free to do what they want. Runners continue receiving the letters R-U-N. Once a runner receives an N, they are out of the game and must help judge or time.

R-U-N Example Activities
Run 100 meters under 14 seconds
Run a 400 meters in 70 to 75 seconds
Run 200 meters in 45 to 46 seconds

Variations: (1) Limit the group to two people and they time each other. (2) Two people work together to perform the activity and both must achieve the stated standard.

Equipment: Each group will need a stopwatch.

Note: This is designed off the game of H-O-R-S-E in basketball.

Check My Speed (with radar gun)

Objective: To determine how fast runners will run by doing a speed check, which determines how far they will run.

Description: After a sufficient warm-up, each runner runs alone for 100 meters and a radar gun is used to measure top speed. Give each runner a recovery period (this can be done while they are waiting for others to go). Each runner runs four times and their speed in miles per hour up is added up to determine how many minutes they will run for the distance workout. If someone runs 16 mph, 15 mph, 14 mph, and 15 mph, that would total 60. Therefore, the distance component of the workout (following the speed check) would be a 60 minute run.

Variations: (1) Vary the number of times a runner runs the speed check to determine how many minutes of distance they run.

Equipment: Radar gun

Note: While running down the road one morning, I noticed the police had set up a portable radar display that indicated how fast cars were traveling down the street. No cars were in sight and it read 12. I realized that was my speed! That day at cross country practice, I took the team over to check our speed and they had a blast. They ran along the side of the road in the park to see what their maximum speed was. They wanted to go over and over again to get a faster and higher speed, and I enthusiastically encouraged them to do so. They were having so much fun; they didn't realize that the faster they ran, the higher their mileage for the day kept rising. It worked out well because the runners that were in better shape ran faster on the radar and therefore had to run longer on the distance run (based upon the above guidelines). You can only hope the police department sets up a radar display in your neighborhood or you can borrow a radar gun from the baseball or softball teams to use.

Move Out and Pick Up

Objective: To run around the track and move out one lane after every lap. As the distance per lap increases the goal is to maintain the same time per lap. This workout challenges the runner to continuously pick up the pace.

Description: Runners will start in lane one of the track and run counter-clockwise. The first lap should be at a slow pace and runners are timed for that lap. After completing the first lap, the runner will move out and run in the second lane. Running in the second lane will cause the runner to run further but they should run it in the same time as the first lap. As the runner continues to move out one lane after finishing each lap, they will continue to run further and a faster pace.

Start the runners at different times to avoid the congestion if they were all to start at the same time.

Track Distance Using a 1 Meter Wide Track Lane	
Lane	Distance
1	400 meters
2	406.3 meters
3	412.56 meters
4	418.85 meters
5	425.1 meters
6	431.4 meters
7	437.7 meters
8	440 meters

Variations: (1) Start in Lane 8 and run very fast to begin with and each lap the pace becomes progressively slower. (2) Run lanes 1-4 and do repeats.(3) Run lane 1 and skip to lane 5 to practice changing from a slow to a fast pace. (4) There are endless combinations of lane movements.

Equipment: stopwatch

Pacer Lights

Objective: To adjust pace based upon feedback given by a teammate.

Description: Form groups of four to six runners of equal running ability in each group. Determine the distance and the pace the group will run at. Determine designated check points where the pace will be indicated. Each group will have one runner with a stopwatch that will be the pace indicator. The pace indicator will not run the interval, but will run to each designated check point. The pace indicator is given the time that should be achieved at each check point. The pace indicator gives a visual signal by dropping their arm or a flag at the designated pace time. This visual signal serves as a check to the runner as to whether they are ahead of pace, on pace, or behind pace. Only the pace indicator is allowed to have a stopwatch. Rotate so that everyone in the group has a chance to be the pace indicator for the group.

Example: A group of five runners will run 5x400 meters in 80 seconds. The designated check point is the 200 meter mark and 400 meter mark. Runner A will be the pace indicator and will cut across to the 200 meter mark and signal by dropping a hand (or flag) when 40 seconds has expired. This will be a visual indicator if they are ahead of, on, or behind pace. Runner A than cuts across infield to the end of the 400 meters and drops a hand or flag as a visual indicator at 80 seconds. After the designated recovery period, Runner A will join the running group and another runner in the group will be the pace indicator.

Variations: (1) The pace indicator runs with the group and drops their hand at the pace time while running.

Equipment: Stopwatch for each group

Note: In the 1970's the International Track Association used pacer lights. These lights were spaced every ten yards along the track. The lights were indicators to both the competitors and the crowd what pace the racers were maintaining.

Tour De France

Description: Set up an interval workout that involves different distances. Each interval would represent a stage of the Tour De France bike race. Keep track of the time for each interval and keep a running total as the workout goes along.

Variations: Include bonus points by winning a stage, i.e., 1st= 15 seconds time deduction, 2nd = 10 seconds time deduction, 3rd = 5 seconds time deduction. To add to the event, include some primes where runners get bonus points (time subtracted) if they are leading at a designated point during the interval.

Equipment: Stopwatch, recording sheet

Tour de France Scoring Sheet			
Athlete Name	Stage 1 Time/ Cumulative Time	Stage 2 Time/ Cumulative Time	Stage 3Time/ Cumulative Time
	/	/	/
	/	/	/
	/	/	/
	/	/	/
	/	/	/

Runner's Pentathlon

Objective: To determine the best all-around runner with a mixture of short and long runs scored decathlon style.

Description: Each runner will compete in five track runs (1500 meters- 400 meters- 800 meters– 200 meters – 3000 meters) with 10-30 minutes recovery time between runs. Points are scored for each run based on the running time with the use of a decathlon scoring type chart (see page 128). With an equal mix of sprints and distance events this challenging competition pits sprinter against distance runner to determine the best all-around track runner. Every runner runs the 1500 meter. Their time is recorded on the scoring chart. Compare the time to the corresponding score on the scoring tables and record their score in points. Give the runners a certain amount of recovery time (15 minutes for workout, 20-30 minutes if you are using it as a competition). Start the next event the 400 meters and time everyone, record on the scoring chart and record the points off the scoring tables. Keep a running cumulative total. After the last event, complete the event by announcing the point totals.

Variations: Use a short version of the Runner's Pentathlon by using half of the distances. 800-200-400-100-1500. In hot weather, the shorter distance is preferred.

Equipment: Scoring chart, scoring tables, stopwatches.

Running Pentathlon Scoring Chart- Long Version: 1500-400-200-800-3000						
Name	1500 time/pts/ cum pts	400 time/pts/ cum pts	200 time/pts/ cum pts	800 time/pts/ cum pts	3000 time/pts/ cum pts	Total Pts/Place
Example	4:59/780/780	1:02/820/1600	29.8/680/2280	2:21/810/3090	10:52/770/3860	3860/3
	/ /	/ /	/ /	/ /	/ /	/ /
	/ /	/ /	/ /	/ /	/ /	/ /
	/ /	/ /	/ /	/ /	/ /	/ /
	/ /	/ /	/ /	/ /	/ /	/ /

Running Pentathlon Scoring Chart- Short Version: 800-200-400-100-1500						
Name	800 time/pts/ cum pts	200 time/pts/ cum pts	400 time/pts/ cum pts	100 time/pts/ cum pts	1500 time/pts/ cum pts	Total Pts/Place
Example	1:59/1170/1170	24.0/1060/2220	58/940/3210	13.6/780/3990	4:40/910/4860	4860/1
	/ /	/ /	/ /	/ /	/ /	/ /
	/ /	/ /	/ /	/ /	/ /	/ /
	/ /	/ /	/ /	/ /	/ /	/ /
	/ /	/ /	/ /	/ /	/ /	/ /

Runner's Pentathlon Scoring Chart

Points	100 meters	200 meters	400 meters	800 meters	1500 meters	3000 meters
1400	9.9	19.78	44.45	1:46.79	3:37.46	7:41.64
1390	9.96	19.9	44.72	1:47.30	3:38.61	7:44.28
1380	10.01	20.02	44.99	1:47.81	3:39.77	7:46.94
1370	10.06	20.14	45.27	1:48.33	3:40.93	7:49.60
1360	10.11	20.26	45.54	1:48.85	3:42.10	7:52.27
1350	10.17	20.38	45.81	1:49.37	3:43.27	7:54.95
1340	10.22	20.5	46.09	1:49.89	3:44.44	7:57.64
1330	10.27	20.62	46.37	1:50.41	3:45.62	8:00.34
1320	10.33	20.74	46.64	1:50.94	3:46.81	8:03.05
1310	10.38	20.86	46.92	1:51.47	3:48.00	8:05.77
1300	10.43	20.99	47.2	1:52.00	3:49.19	8:08.50
1290	10.49	21.11	47.48	1:52.53	3:50.39	8:11.24
1280	10.54	21.23	47.76	1:53.06	3:51.59	8:14.00
1270	10.6	21.36	48.05	1:53.60	3:52.80	8:16.76
1260	10.65	21.48	48.33	1:54.14	3:54.01	8:19.53
1250	10.71	21.61	48.62	1:54.68	3:55.22	8:22.32
1240	10.76	21.73	48.9	1:55.22	3:56.45	8:25.11
1230	10.82	21.86	49.19	1:55.76	3:57.67	8:27.92
1220	10.87	21.99	49.48	1:56.31	3:58.90	8:30.74
1210	10.93	22.12	49.77	1:56.86	4:00.14	8:33.57
1200	10.99	22.24	50.06	1:57.41	4:01.38	8:36.41
1190	11.04	22.37	50.35	1:57.96	4:02.63	8:39.27
1180	11.1	22.5	50.64	1:58.52	4:03.88	8:42.13
1170	11.16	22.63	50.94	1:59.08	4:05.14	8:45.01
1160	11.21	22.76	51.23	1:59.64	4:06.40	8:47.90
1150	11.27	22.89	51.53	2:00.20	4:07.67	8:50.81
1140	11.33	23.02	51.83	2:00.77	4:08.94	8:53.72
1130	11.39	23.15	52.03	2:01.34	4:10.22	8:56.63
1120	11.44	23.29	52.43	2:01.91	4:11.51	8:59.59
1110	11.5	23.42	52.73	2:02.48	4:12.80	9:02.55
1100	11.56	23.55	53.04	2:03.06	4:14.09	9:05.52
1090	11.62	23.69	53.34	2:03.63	4:15.40	9:08.52
1080	11.68	23.82	53.65	2:04.22	4:16.71	9:11.49
1070	11.74	23.96	53.95	2:04.80	4:18.02	9:14.50
1060	11.8	24.09	54.26	2:05.39	4:19.34	9:17.53
1050	11.86	24.23	54.57	2:05.97	4:20.67	9:20.56
1040	11.92	24.37	54.89	2:06.57	4:22.00	9:23.62
1030	11.98	24.5	55.2	2:07.16	4:23.34	9:26.68
1020	12.04	24.64	55.52	2:07.76	4:24.69	9:29.76
1010	12.1	24.78	55.83	2:08.36	4:26.04	9:32.86
1000	12.16	24.92	56.15	2:08.96	4:27.40	9:35.97
990	12.23	25.06	56.47	2:09.57	4:28.77	9:39.10
980	12.29	25.2	56.79	2:10.18	4:30.14	9:42.25
970	12.35	25.35	57.12	2:10.79	4:31.52	9:45.41
960	12.41	25.49	57.44	2:11.41	4:32.91	9:48.58
950	12.48	25.63	57.77	2:12.03	4:34.30	9:51.77
940	12.54	25.78	58.1	2:12:65	4:35.70	9:54.98
930	12.6	25.92	58.43	2:13.28	4:37.11	9:58.21
920	12.67	26.07	58.76	2:13.91	4:38.53	10:01.46

Runner's Pentathlon Scoring Chart

Points	100 meters	200 meters	400 meters	800 meters	1500 meters	3000 meters
910	12.73	26.22	59.09	2:14.54	4:39.96	10:04.72
900	12.8	26.36	59.43	2:15.17	4:41.39	10:08.00
890	12.86	26.51	59.77	2:15.81	4:42.83	10:11.30
880	12.93	26.66	1:00.10	2:16.64	4:44.28	10:14.61
870	12.99	26.81	1:00.45	2:17.10	4:45.74	10:17.95
860	13.06	26.96	1:00.79	2:17.76	4:47.20	10:21.30
850	13.13	27.11	1:01.13	2:18.41	4:48.68	10:24.68
840	13.19	27.27	1:01.48	2:19.07	4:50.16	10:28.07
830	13.26	27.42	1:01.83	2:19.73	4:51.65	10:31.49
820	13.33	27.57	1:02.18	2:20.40	4:53.15	10:34.92
810	13.4	27.73	1:02.54	2:21.07	4:54.66	10:38.38
800	13.47	27.89	1:02.89	2:21.74	4:56.18	10:41.85
790	13.54	28.04	1:03.25	2:22.42	4:57.71	10:45.35
780	13.61	28.2	1:03.61	2:23.10	4:59.25	10:48.88
770	13.68	28.36	1:03.97	2:23.79	5:00.79	10:52.42
760	13.75	28.52	1:04.34	2:24.48	5:02.35	10:55.99
750	13.82	28.68	1:04.71	2:25.18	5:03.92	10:59.58
740	13.89	28.85	1:05.08	2:25.88	5:05.50	11:03.19
730	13.96	29.01	1:05.45	2:26.59	5:07.09	11:06.83
720	14.03	29.18	1:05.82	2:27.30	5:08.69	11:10.50
710	14.11	29.34	1:06.20	2:28.01	5:10.30	11:14.19
700	14.18	29.51	1:06.58	2:28.73	5:11.93	11:17.90
690	14.25	29.68	1:06.96	2:29.46	5:13.56	11:21.65
680	14.33	29.85	1:07.35	2:30.19	5:15.21	11:25.42
670	14.4	30.02	1:07.74	2:30.93	5:16.87	11:29.21
660	14.48	30.19	1:08.13	2:31.67	5:18.54	11:33.04
650	14.55	30.36	1:08.52	2:32.42	5:20.22	11:36.89
640	14.63	30.54	1:08.92	2:33.17	5:21.92	11:40.78
630	14.71	30.71	1:09.32	2:33.93	5:23.63	11:44.69
620	14.79	30.89	1:09.73	2:34.70	5:25.35	11:48.64
610	14.87	31.07	1:10.13	2:35.47	5:27.09	11:52.62
600	14.94	31.25	1:10.54	2:36.25	5:28.84	11:56.63
590	15.02	31.43	1:10.96	2:37.03	5:30.61	12:00.68
580	15.11	31.62	1:11.37	2:37.82	5:32.29	12:04.76
570	15.19	31.8	1:11.80	2:38.62	5:34.19	12:08.87
560	15.27	31.99	1:12.22	2:39.42	5:36.00	12:13.02
550	15.35	32.18	1:12.65	2:40.24	5:37.83	12:17.21
540	15.43	32.37	1:13.08	2:41.06	5:39.68	12:21.44
530	15.52	32.56	1:13.52	2:41.88	5:41.54	12:25.70
520	15.6	32.75	1:13.96	2:42.72	5:43.43	12:30.01
510	15.69	32.95	1:14.40	2:43.56	5:45.32	12:34.36
500	15.78	33.15	1:14.85	2:44.41	5:47.24	12:38.75
490	15.86	33.35	1:15.31	2:45.27	5:49.18	12:43.18
480	15.95	33.55	1:15.76	2:46.16	5:51.14	12:47.66
470	16.04	33.75	1:16.23	2:47.02	5:53.11	12:52.19
460	16.13	33.96	1:16.70	2:47.91	5:55.11	12:56.77
450	16.22	31.17	1:17.17	2:48.81	5:57.13	13:01.39
440	16.32	34.38	1:17.65	2:49.71	5:59.18	13:06.07
430	16.41	34.59	1:18.13	2:50.63	6:01.24	13:10.80

Runner's Pentathlon Scoring Chart

Points	100 meters	200 meters	400 meters	800 meters	1500 meters	3000 meters
420	16.51	34.8	1:18.62	2:51.56	6:03.33	13:15.59
410	16.6	35.02	1:19.12	2:52.50	6:05.45	13:20.43
400	16.7	35.24	1:19.62	2:53.45	6:07.59	13:25.33
390	16.8	35.47	1:20.13	2:54.41	6:09.76	13:30.30
380	16.9	35.69	1:20.64	2:55.39	6:11.96	13:35.32
370	17	35.92	1:21.16	2:56.38	6:14.18	13:40.42
360	17.1	36.15	1:21.69	2:57.38	6:16.44	13:45.58
350	17.2	36.39	1:22.23	2:58.39	6:18.73	13:50.82
340	17.31	36.63	1:22.77	2:59.42	6:21.05	13:56.13
330	17.41	36.87	1:23.32	3:00.47	6:23.40	14:01.52
320	17.52	37.12	1:23.88	3:01.53	6:25.79	14:07.00
310	17.63	37.37	1:24.45	3:02.61	6:28.22	14:12.56
300	17.74	37.62	1:25.03	3:03.71	6:30.69	14:18.21
290	17.86	37.88	1:25.62	3:04.82	6:33.20	14:23.95
280	17.97	38.14	1:26.21	3:05.95	6:35.75	14:29.80
270	18.09	38.41	1:26.82	3:07.11	6:38.35	14:35.75
260	18.21	38.68	1:27.44	3:08.28	6:41.00	14:41.81
250	18.33	39.96	1:28.08	3:09.48	6:43.70	14:47.99
240	18.46	39.25	1:28.72	3:10.70	6:46.45	14:54.29
230	18.58	39.53	1:29.38	3:11.95	6:49.27	15:00.73
220	18.71	39.83	1:30.05	3:13.23	6:52.14	15:07.31
210	18.85	40.13	1:30.74	3:14.53	6:55.08	15:14.04
200	18.98	40.44	1:31.45	3:15.87	6:58.09	15:20.93
190	19.12	40.76	1:32.17	3:17.24	7:01.18	15:27.99
180	19.27	41.09	1:32.91	3:18.65	7:04.35	15:35.25
170	19.41	41.42	1:33.67	3:20.10	7:07.60	15:42.71
160	19.57	41.77	1:34.46	3:21.59	7:10.96	15:50.39
150	19.72	42.13	1:35.27	3:23.12	7:14.42	15:58.32
140	19.88	42.49	1:36.11	3:24.71	7:18.00	16:06.51
130	20.05	42.88	1:36.98	3:26.36	7:21.71	16:15.00
120	20.23	43.27	1:37.88	3:28.07	7:25.57	16:23.83
110	20.41	43.69	1:38.82	3:29.86	7:29.59	16:33.03
100	20.6	44.12	1:39.81	3:31.72	7:33.80	16:42.67
90	20.8	44.58	1:40.85	3:33.69	7:38.22	16:52.79
80	21.01	45.06	1:41.94	3:35.77	7:42.90	17:03.50
70	21.24	45.57	1:43.11	3:37.98	7:47.88	17:14.90
60	21.48	46.12	1:44.36	3:40.35	7:52.23	17:27.15
50	21.74	46.72	1:45.72	3:42.94	7:59.04	17:40.46
40	22.03	47.38	1:47.23	3:45.79	8:05.48	17:55.19
30	22.36	48.14	1:48.94	3:49.04	8:12.78	18:11.92
20	22.76	49.03	1:50.97	3:52.88	8:21.45	18:31.75
10	23.27	50.19	1:53.62	3:57.90	8:32.74	18:57.60
0	24.5	53	2:00.00	4:10.00	9:00.00	20:00.00

References

Anderson, E. (1996). *Training Games: Coaching Runners Creatively.* TAFNewsPress:Mountain View, CA.

Anderson, E. & Hibbert, A. (2006).*Training Games Coaching & Racing Creatively,* 4th ed. TAFNews Press: Mountain View, CA.

Hinson, C. (1995).*Fitness for Children.* Human Kinetics: Champaign, IL.

Karp, J. (2010). *101 Developmental Concepts and Workouts for Cross Country Runners.* Monterey, CA: Coaches Choice

Moving into the Future: National Standards for Physical Education, 2nd Edition. (2004). Reston,VA: NASPE National Association for Sport and Physical Education.

Pangrazi, R. (2001). *Dynamic Physical Education for Elementary School Children,* Allyn and Bacon, Boston, MA.

Peck, S. (2007). *101 Fun, Creative and Interactive Games for Kids.* Healthy Learning: Monterey CA.

Quality Coaches, Quality Sports: National Standards for Athletic Coaches, (1995). Reston, VA: NASPE National Association for Sport and Physical Education.

Quality Coaches, Quality Sports: National Standards for Sport Coaches, 2nd Edition. (2006). Reston,VA: NASPE National Association for Sport and Physical Education.

About the Author

Dr. Mark Stanbrough is a professor in the Department of Health, Physical Education and Recreation at Emporia State University in Kansas. He teaches graduate and undergraduate exercise physiology and sports psychology classes and is the director of Coaching Education. The Coaching Education program at Emporia State is currently one of only ten universities in the United States to be accredited by the National Council for the Accreditation of Coaching Education. He was a co-founder of the online physical education graduate program, the first in the United States to go completely online. He received his Ph.D. in exercise physiology from the University of Oregon, and undergraduate and master's degrees from Emporia State in physical education. He has served as department chair and has served on the National Association for Sport and Physical Education National Sport Steering Committee and is a past member of the board of directors for the National Council for the Accreditation of Coaching Education.

Mark has over thirty years of coaching experience at the collegiate, high school, middle school and club level. Coach Stanbrough served eight years as the head men's and women's cross country/track and field coach at Emporia State (1984-1992) with the 1986 women's cross country team finishing second at the NAIA national meet. He has also coached at Emporia High School and Glasco High School in Kansas. He is a Level I and II USATF certified coach. Mark has served as the USATF Missouri Valley Association President and as the head referee at numerous national meets. He is a member of the Emporia State University Athletic Hall of Honor and the Health, Physical Education, Recreation Hall of Honor and has won numerous coach-of-the-year awards at the high school and collegiate levels.

Printed in Great Britain
by Amazon